Study Guide to

The Water Dancer

A Novel

by

Ta-Nehisi Coates

by Ray Moore

D1522439

Contents

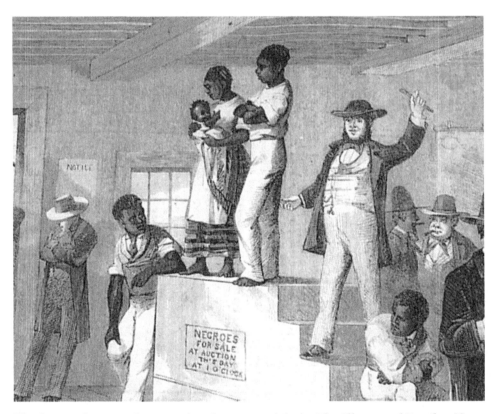

The image shows a slave auction from an article in *The Illustrated London News* of February 16th, 1861, on slave auctions in Richmond, Virginia. This detail from a larger engraving shows a family, including a baby in the mother's arms, on the auction block. This image is in the public domain. Source: Wikimedia Commons.

Preface

A study guide is an *aid* to the close reading of a text; it is *never* a substitute for reading the text itself. This novel deserves to be read *reflectively*, and the aim of this guide is to facilitate such a reading.

The Guide to the Novel section includes at least one question for each chapter. These questions aim to focus the reader's attention on important issues. Some questions are carefully worded to draw your attention to important aspects of the text which you need to understand. Other questions are very open-ended: they are not designed to lead you in any direction, but simply to elicit your ideas. It should always be clear to you which type of question you are being asked. The questions do not normally have simple answers, nor is there always one answer. Readers can use these questions individually or in groups; responses may be in writing (e.g., a reading journal), discussion (e.g., a reading circle), an individual or group presentation, or in the form of quiet individual reflection.

None of these questions has answers provided. This is a deliberate choice. The questions are for readers who want to come to their own conclusions about the text and not simply to be told what to think about it by someone else. Even 'suggested' answers would limit the exploration of the text by readers themselves which is the primary aim of the questions. In the classroom, I found that students frequently came up with answers that I had not even considered, and, not infrequently, that they expressed their ideas better than I could have done. The point of this guide is to open up the text, not to close it down by providing 'ready-made answers.'

The Notes that accompany selected chapters briefly explain the most important names, and cultural and historical references used in the text. The Summary sections provide a condensed version of the main plot and character developments, and the Analysis sections give a commentary on the most significant points of each chapter. The commentaries do not set out directly to answer the guiding questions, but they sometimes do cover the same ground, and therefore I urge readers *not* to move on to them until they have carefully considered the guiding questions and come to their own conclusions. The commentaries represent my best understanding of the text at this point in time. They make no claim to be complete and certainly not to be definitive. Feel free to disagree.

Acknowledgements

As always, I am indebted to the work of numerous reviewers and critics. Where I am conscious of having taken an idea or a phrase from a particular author, I have cited the source in the text and the bibliography. Any failure to do so is an omission which I will be happy to correct if it is drawn to my attention. I believe that all quotations used fall under the definition of 'fair use.' If I am in error on any quotation, I will immediately correct it. Please note that this guide and the novel are written in American English, but some of the works quoted were originally written in Standard English – the most obvious difference is the spelling.

A Study Guide

Thanks are due to my wife, Barbara, for reading the manuscript, for offering valuable suggestions, and for putting the text into the correct formats for publication. Any errors which remain are my own.

Spoiler alert!

If you are reading the novel for the first time, you may wish to go straight to the Guide to the Novel section and consult the other sections later since they do explain everything that happens in the novel, including the ending. Of course, you are free to read this guide in any order you want to.

Introduction

Plot Summary

The main action of the novel takes place in the mid-1850s. Hiram is the mixed-race son of Howell Walker, the master of Lockless Plantation in Virginia, and Rose, who was once a slave on that plantation. As the soil in Old Virginia becomes exhausted by the intensive monoculture of tobacco, so the prosperity of earlier days is ebbing away, and the plantation owners feel themselves increasingly driven to sell their slaves down South to make up the lost revenue. Thus, it is that Rose is sold when Hiram is a child, and this experience is so traumatic that Hiram, who in other respects has a photographic memory, represses all recollection of her. He is brought up by an old woman, Thena, all of whose own children have been sold Natchez-way by the master. When he is called to work in the mansion, Hiram hopes that his father will recognize his intelligence and allow him to inherit Lockless rather than Howell's one legitimate, white son, Maynard who is very obviously unsuited to and ill-equipped for the challenge. However, Howell's plan is to give Hiram just sufficient education for him to be able to serve and to guide the socially awkward and foolish Maynard. These plans come to nothing when a carriage Hiram is driving in a storm plunges off the bridge over Goose River, and Maynard is drowned. This dramatic incident opens the narrative.

Eventually, Hiram realizes that Howell will never let him inherit Lockless and decides to run away. He seeks the help of Georgie Parks, a free black man who is rumored to have connections with the Underground Railroad. However, Parks betrays Hiram and the young woman, Sophia, with whom he is escaping, and both are captured. Eventually, after a great deal of suffering, Hiram is liberated by Corrine Quinn a young woman who appears to be one of the Virginia Quality but is actually an important agent for the Underground Railroad. Hiram moves north to Philadelphia to work for the Railroad and there he meets and goes on a mission with the legendary Harriet Tubman, known to all as Moses.

What Hiram and Harriet have in common is the power of Conduction; that is, the ability to travel almost instantaneously over large distances. The difference is that Harriet can control this power while Hiram is simply subject to it. On several occasions, he has been teleported short distances, most obviously on the night he almost drowned in the River Goose when he found himself teleported out of the river and into a field more than a mile away from the bank. Slowly, Hiram begins to understand that Conduction is linked to recovering the lost memories of his mother, Rose.

Hiram is called back to Virginia by Corrine who asks him to return to Lockless as Howell's personal servant (and slave) because in that position he will be able to feed the Underground valuable intelligence about the plantation. He agrees to do this if Corrine commits to helping Thena and Sophia escape to the free states in the North. When Hiram returns to Lockless, Howell gives him an emotional welcome. Although he has only been away for a year, the plantation is in a significantly worse state, and there are very few slaves left.

Hiram reunites with Thena, to whom he apologizes for the harsh words he used to her before his escape. He also finds Sophia at Lockless. She has a baby called Caroline (Carrie) who is Nathaniel Howell's daughter. For some time, Hiram finds it hard to accept that the woman he loves has had a baby with another man, even one who raped her, but he finally understands that he has no right to dictate to Sophia. Hiram becomes his father's servant and companion. Howell confesses to him that he regrets many of the things he has done in his life and hints that he plans to have Hiram manage the plantation after he dies. Looking through the ledgers, Hiram learns that Lockless is deeply in debt and that Howell owes his brother Nathaniel a lot of money.

At this time, Hiram is grappling with three difficult issues. He is still trying to understand the nature of Conduction so as to be able to control it; he is trying to come to terms with Sophia's determination not to become the possession of any man ever again; and he is trying to put aside the fact that Carrie is another man's child and accept her as his own.

Sophia becomes more worried that Nathaniel intends to take her away to Tennessee where he might legally marry her. Then, Thena is robbed of all the money she has been saving to buy her freedom from Howell. Thus, when Corrine Quinn comes to Lockless for Christmas, Hiram insists that she arrange to have Sophia, Carrie and Thena conducted out of Elm County to freedom. Corrine reassures him that she has bought Sophia from Nathaniel and that she is therefore safe. She tells him that the Underground cannot get them North yet because doing so would compromise bigger plans. Hiram resolves to use the power of Conduction, which he now believes he has learned to control, to get them to Philadelphia, but when he tells Sophia, she refuses to leave without him, and when he tells Thena about having met her daughter, Kessiah, and promised to reunite them, she reacts with anger and rejection.

So far, Hiram has only managed to achieve Conduction over small distances; in order to conduct Thena to safety, he knows that he will need a deeper memory and an object associated with that memory. Searching Howell's highboy, he finds a shell necklace that his mother, Rose, gave him the day she was sold. This triggers the memories of his mother that he has so long repressed: Rose tried to run away with Hiram, and was on the run for three days before they were caught, and Howell sold her as punishment.

Thena explains to Hiram that her angry outburst was caused by her enormous pain. Soon after, Hiram conducts Thena to Philadelphia, where she is met by Kessiah and Harriet. Hiram immediately returns, but wakes to find himself in the care of Corrine and Hawkins at the Starfall inn.

That fall, Howell dies and Hiram learns that Corrine has taken responsibility for Howell's debts in return for ownership of the plantation on his death. The few slaves are sent safely North and replaced by agents, and Lockless becomes an

Underground station, which Hiram manages. He and Sophia stay in Elm County, stay as slaves, and continue their work for the Underground.

Why Read this Book

There are, of course, many slave narratives written by people who actually were slaves. Among many others, I will mention: Frederick Douglass, *Narrative of the Life of Frederick Douglass, an American Slave* (Boston, 1845); Solomon Northup, *Twelve Years a Slave* (Auburn, and Buffalo, New York and London, 1853); and Harriet Jacobs, *Incidents in the Life of a Slave Girl* (Boston, 1861). There are also many novels that tell the story of slavery perhaps the most famous being Harriet Beecher Stowe, *Uncle Tom's Cabin; or, Life Among the Lowly* (Boston, 1852).

What Coates does, however, is something that none of these narratives could possibly have done: he writes a fictional slave narrative that is relevant to America Today – an America where Black Lives Matter and the Me Too Movement are in conflict with White Supremacist groups and a power structure still dominated by men.

Ta-Nehisi Coates is one of the most important Black voices in America today. Dwight Garner writes, "Over the past decade, Ta-Nehisi Coates has emerged as an important public intellectual and perhaps America's most incisive thinker about race." He is the author of *Between the World and Me: Notes on the First 150 Years in America* (2015) and *We Were Eight Years in Power: An American Tragedy* (2017). He is also the author of the article, "The Case for Reparations: Two hundred fifty years of slavery. Ninety years of Jim Crow. Sixty years of separate but equal. Thirty-five years of racist housing policy. Until we reckon with our compounding moral debts, America will never be whole" which appeared in *The Atlantic* (June 2014), and of "The Black Family in the Age of Mass Incarceration" in *The Atlantic* (Oct. 2015). I recommend that you read them all.

Issues with this Text

There is no explicit sex in the novel and no graphic violence. Coates evidently took a decision to concentrate on the more subtle, psychological wounds of slavery rather than the obvious, and very real, physical brutalities. Perhaps even more surprisingly, there is no language that could offend anyone. The narrative is not littered with cuss-words nor with the n-word, both being used sparingly.

What the novel *does do* is challenge America's collective amnesia about slavery and its collective desire to relegate it to the past and to deny its relevance to the present. I imagine that readers who support keeping statues of white Civil War heroes in the South would be resistant to reading the novel in the first place and to accepting its ideas even if they did.

Terms Used in the Novel

Coates uses a number of terms in the novel that are his invention rather than in common usage. The term 'Underground Railroad', for example, is historical. It began to be used in the early 1830s and quickly spawned related euphemisms: the homes and businesses that harbored runaways were called 'stations' or 'depots'; those who ran them were 'stationmasters'; those who moved the fugitives from one station to the next were 'conductors'; and people who contributed money or goods to support the cause were 'stockholders'. Coates uses most of these terms in the novel ('stockholders' being the one exception), but he also uses words to which he gives his own meaning. Beth Mowbray explain that this "expands the pre-existing meaning of the old language, removing common assumptions and leaving the reader open to be influenced by Coates, to view his characters through a different lens."

The Quality refers to the plantation-owning class of Old Virginia whose wealth is built on the ownership of slaves who toil in the tobacco fields. Hiram writes, "I was just beginning to understand the great valley separating the Quality and the Tasked – that the Tasked, hunched low in the fields, carrying the tobacco from hillock to hogshead, led backbreaking lives and that the Quality who lived in the house high above … did not" (19). The Quality in Virginia, both men and women, dress elegantly, live in luxury, and pride themselves on their good manners. This is, however, a thin and brittle veneer. As soon as they begin drinking, they reveal themselves to be ill-mannered, foul-mouthed and brutal. The 1850s is a period of increasing economic depression in Virginia. The Quality have impoverished the land through excessive planting of tobacco, and as a result their income is falling. Many are moving further West looking for virgin soil, and those that remain make up the shortfall in their income by selling their slaves to pay their debts.

The Low refers to poor whites who work and live in terrible conditions hardly better than the slaves they despise. They might normally be called 'poor whites' or even 'white trash' – think of Bob Ewell in *To Kill a Mockingbird* (1960) by Harper Lee. There are really no significant characters in the novel who fall into this social group, since neither the Quality nor the Tasked mix with them. One paradox that is explored in the novel is the fact that the Low, who have so much in common with the Tasked, do not identify with them and join forces against the Quality. This is because the Low cling onto their whiteness as the one thing that differentiates them from the black slaves. This myth of white racial purity is fostered by the Quality as an effective control mechanism. Hiram comments of the Low, "They were a degraded and downtrodden nation enduring the boot of the Quality, solely for the right to put a boot of their own to the Tasked" (52).

The Tasked refers to enslaved black people. Its use is largely confined to parts of the narrative set in Virginia where it is used as a convenient euphemism to hide the cruel realities of enslavement. The Quality delude themselves into thinking that they treat their blacks well and that they are happy in their condition. **The Task** is the term used to describe the institution of slavery and also units of slave laborers.

The Coffin is a phrase used by many of the enslaved to describe states where slavery exists legally, particularly those in the Deep South where the conditions in which slaves live and toil are notoriously hard.

Ryland's Hounds is a collective term for slave catchers both in Elm County and beyond. The name comes from Ryland's Jail in Starfall, which is in turn named for the man who runs the jail where runaways are imprisoned. Slave catchers are prevalent in the South, and, to a lesser extent, the North. Their role is to discourage slaves from trying to escape in the first place by setting an example of the brutal treatment they will receive when recaptured.

Conduction is the paranormal power of teleportation possessed by many Africans in the past (e.g., the African King and Santi Bess) and some African-Americans in the present (e.g., Harriet Tubman and Hiram Walker). Individuals use vivid memories and contact with water to generate a blue light that lifts and carries them instantly over both short and long distances. The implication of the novel is that this ability was once fairly common to pure blooded Africans, and that those enslaved black people who jumped into the ocean from the decks of slave ships did not drown but used Conduction to return to their homelands. Inevitably, as Africans in America lose contact with their oral history and culture, Conduction becomes rarer.

Family Trees

Key: = indicates legal marriage; - indicates informal union.

The Walker Family of Lockless

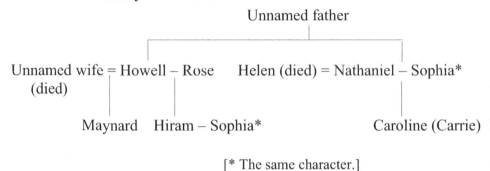

Unnamed father

Unnamed wife = Howell – Rose   Helen (died) = Nathaniel – Sophia*
   (died)

           Maynard   Hiram – Sophia*   Caroline (Carrie)

[* The same character.]

Hiram's Family on his Mother's Side

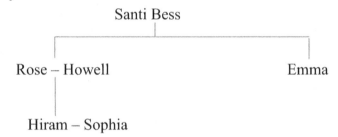

Santi Bess

Rose – Howell   Emma

Hiram – Sophia

The Tubman Family (as it appears in the novel)

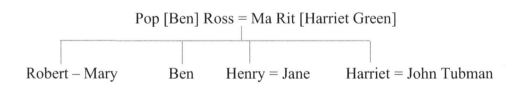

Pop [Ben] Ross = Ma Rit [Harriet Green]

Robert – Mary   Ben   Henry = Jane   Harriet = John Tubman

The Water Dancer by Ta-Nehisi Coates

Significant Characters

The Walker Family:

Howell Walker is Hiram's father and the slave-owning master of the tobacco plantation called Lockless. Howell's marriage produced one legitimate son, Maynard (who is thus Hiram's half-brother). At the start of the novel Howell is around seventy and a widower. In a relationship that seems to have been similar to that between Thomas Jefferson and his slave Sally Hemings, Howell had some emotional attachment to the beautiful Rose (Hiram's mother) and convinced himself that his feelings were returned. Roses' attempt to escape with her son stripped from their relationship the gentile pretentions in which he had shrouded it, and that is why he was so angry and vindictive toward her. As an old man, Howell expresses his regret to Hiram for some of his actions, and confesses that he is not a good person. However, he continues to see himself as a helpless victim trapped by the nature of the racist society in which he lived, and right up to the end, he takes no action to right his wrongs. Shaun McMichael comments:

> In the depiction of Walker, Coates incarnates Toni Morrison's idea put forth in *Playing the Dark: Whiteness and the Literary Imagination* (Harvard University Press, 1992), in which she posits that racist whites without slaves to domineer dissolve into ineffectuality and incoherence. Walker prefers to nurse falsehoods about his white son Maynard's abilities, rather than see Hiram's inherent worth and potential; to acknowledge Hiram as the obvious choice as inheritor of his business would be to admit the hollow conceit of race underpinning Walker's crumbling world.

Nathaniel Walker is Howell's brother, though he never actually appears in the narrative. He owns a plantation close to Lockless but spends increasing amounts of his time in Tennessee – part of a general movement of Virginia planters to the West in order to find more fertile land. He is the person who owns Sophia, but he cannot bring himself to have her live on his property, so he has arranged with his brother for her to live at Lockless. Each weekend, she is brought to his mansion dressed in fine clothes, and he has sex with her – an example of institutionalized rape. Eventually, Sophia becomes pregnant and gives birth to a girl (Caroline). Although he is the child's biological father, he takes no interest in her.

Helen Walker was Nathaniel's wife who died in childbirth before the main action of the novel begins. She and Sophia were raised together and became best friends in childhood. However, their relationship changed when they grew up and Sophia became Helen's enslaved maid.

Maynard is Howell Walker's only legitimate, white child and therefore the legal heir to Lockless despite being intellectually and temperamentally unsuitable. Knowing Maynard to be childish, extravagant and irresponsible, when they are both young teens, Howell assigns Hiram to be Maynard's personal manservant.

9

Despite all the care that Hiram takes to protect his half-brother, Maynard, being vulgar and rude, fond of heavy drinking, gambling away too much money, and frequenting brothels, never fits in with Virginia high society. The Virginia Quality literally, "turned their backs on him … He was what he would always be [to them] – Maynard the Goof, Maynard the Lame, Maynard the Fool, the apple who'd fallen many miles from the tree" (5). He is killed when Hiram accidentally crashes the carriage in which Maynard is riding into the River Goose. Maynard, who had failed to learn to swim despite Hiram's efforts to teach him when they were younger, drowns. Hiram feels that his half-brother is an extreme case that illustrates the way in which slavery weakens the white, master class: always reliant on their black slaves to do the hard work (and more surprisingly) the hard thinking, the whites are often incapable of doing either for themselves. Without their slaves, they are virtually helpless. Hiram reflects on Maynard's death, "slavery murdered him … slavery made a child of him." As Maynard desperately calls, "'Please!'" to Hiram, Hiram reflects bitterly, "I had never before recalled him speaking in a manner that reflected the true nature of our positions" (7). At the time of his death, Maynard is engaged to Corrine Quinn, a rich young Virginia heiress.

The Biological Family of the Protagonist/Narrator:

Santi Bess, Hiram's grandmother, was a "pure-blood African" who in the distant past led forty-eight enslaved blacks from Lockless Plantation to freedom (279). According to legend, she took them down to the River Goose into which they walked and reemerged in Africa. Hiram, a rationalist by education, doubts this story but finally he comes to understand that it really happened.

Rose, Hiram's beautiful mother, was a slave on Lockless who was raped by Howell Walker, the man who owned her. She attempted to run away with her nine-year old son, and in retribution Howell sold her for a horse, separating her from Hiram forever. From Thena, Hiram learns that his mother was, "*A beautiful woman, the kindest heart, did not gossip, kept to herself*" (19). She was the water dancer. What happened to her is not known.

Emma was Rose's sister and thus Hiram's aunt. He remembers that she and his mother would water dance together, but when tobacco yields started falling, Emma was one of the first of the Tasked sold down Natchez way by Howell.

Hiram, the protagonist and narrator, is nineteen at the start of the novel. He is born into slavery on Lockless plantation (c.1834) as the result of his mother's rape by the master. Hiram is nine years old when Howell sells Rose, and from the time of that traumatic event, he has repressed all memory of her and can only reconstruct details about her from what others tell him. Hiram is taken in by Thena, a sad and bitter old woman all of whose children have been sold by Howell. She becomes his surrogate mother. Without his biological mother, Hiram looks to his white father for approval and for a sense of family. He realizes at the age of five that he has a photographic memory and a fine intelligence, and for many years, he cherishes the delusional hope that his father will free him and even leave Lockless to him rather than to Maynard. Wamuwi Mbao points to the protagonist's divided consciousness, "Hiram's fatal flaw is to regard himself as independent, and the curdling realization that follows is that he is as much part of Lockless's property as the shining house on the hill. He is caught between the false consciousness of the Quality and the burning awareness that being Tasked means occupying a world where being exceptional counts for nothing." The day after his mother is forcibly taken from him, Hiram experiences his first Conduction (a paranormal capability in which the power of memory is used to travel through space-time). His second experience of Conduction occurs when he comes close to drowning in the River Goose. He sees visions of his ancestors and of a woman he recognizes as his mother water dancing, and wakes to find himself in a field some distance from the river. For the rest of the novel, Hiram works to understand exactly what Conduction is and how he can control the power that he has in order to use it to free enslaved people.

The Tasked on Lockless:

Thena is an old slave woman at Lockless who has a reputation for being mean, though Hiram "had heard that Thena had not always been this way, that in another life, one lived right here on the Street, she was a mother not just to five children of her own but to all the children of the Street" (14). When Hiram is effectively orphaned at the age of nine following the sale of his mother, Thena takes him in. Hiram chooses to live with her because he instinctively understands that she is heartbroken by the pain she has suffered, "I sensed the depth of that loss, her pain, a rage she, unlike the rest of us, refused to secret away, and I found that rage to be true and correct" (15). Eventually, Hiram learns "the precise root of her rage" (15): she lost her husband, Big John to fever and had her five children (Silas, Claire, Aram, Alice, and Kessiah) sold down South. She shows herself to be extremely caring and loyal, and to repay her Hiram wants to reunite Thena with one of her daughters, Kessiah. When he first tells her, Thena is afraid of the pain that will resurface if she sees Kessiah again, but she finally agrees. Hiram conducts her to Philadelphia, where she spends the final years of her life living in freedom with Kessiah.

Big John, Thena's husband, was the field driver on Lockless, but he died years before the action of the novel begins. Thena tells Hiram that her husband was appointed the driver by Howell, "'because he was the wisest – wiser than any of them whites, and their whole lives depended on him … Weren't nobody who knew more about the ways and knacks of the golden leaf than my man" (17). She is convinced that the declining yield and income from tobacco on Lockless would not have happened but for his passing.

Boss Harlan is the man now in Big John's place. He is, "a low white who meted out 'correction' when it was deemed appropriate … the enforcer of Lockless … presiding over the fields" (12).

Roscoe is Howell's long-serving personal servant. He dies while Hiram is living in Philadelphia and this creates an opening for Corrine Quinn to insert Hiram into Lockless in order to gain information about the state of the plantation.

Ella is the highly-skilled head cook at Lockless until she is suddenly sold.

Sophia is a beautiful young black slave living at Lockless, though she is owned by Nathaniel Walker, Howell's brother. She was born and raised in Carolina, where she was in a happy relationship with a man named Mercury. After being sold, she was brought to Lockless. Nathaniel Walker establishes her as his mistress; he regularly rapes her and eventually fathers her baby, Caroline (Carrie). Hiram loves Sophia and she has feelings for him, but she is fiercely independent. She resists the idea of escaping the oppression of slavery only to become the possession of a husband, but eventually agrees to be with Hiram because she freely chose to be so.

Other Characters in Elm County:

Ryland is the name of leading slavecatcher in Elm County who oversees Ryland's Jail in Starfall where runaway slaves and slaves about to be sold are confined. His name is used by the Tasked as a generic term for all slave catchers who are referred to as Ryland's Hounds.

Georgie Parks is a black man who bought his freedom in the days when that was still possible. He lives with his family in Freetown, an all-black suburb of Starfall. Like Big John, he "seemed to have a preternatural understanding of agriculture and all its cycles," and had warned of the danger of soil impoverishment due to tobacco monoculture (55). He is widely-respected for his intelligence amongst both blacks and whites. Many black people believe that Georgie is secretly connected to the Underground Railway, and though he has only a vague and, as it turns out, inaccurate, conception of what the Underground is, Hiram asks Georgie to help him and Sophia to escape. Georgie tries very hard to dissuade Hiram, but finally he reluctantly agrees. However, he betrays Hiram and Sophia to Ryland's Hounds leading to their capture and imprisonment. Georgie's motivation is complex. As a free black man, his position is very vulnerable, and he seeks to protect his family by collaborating with the slave catchers. Later, Corrine takes revenge against him. It is not entirely clear what form this takes but when Hiram visits Freetown about a year after his failed escape attempt, he finds the suburb deserted and Georgie's house a burnt-out wreck.

Amber Parks is Georgie's wife with whom he has a baby son.

Alice Caulley is a member of the Quality who attends a social gathering at Lockless where she shows herself to be vulgar and cruel.

Members of the Virginia Underground Railroad:

Corrine Quinn is a wealthy young white woman who owns the rich plantation of Bryceton not far from Lockless. To all appearances, she is the epitome of Virginia Quality, but in reality, she is an abolitionist and a covert operative of the

Underground Railway of which Bryceton is an important station. Her hatred of slavery is so visceral that she exerts total control over her agents and is prepared to use people quite ruthlessly in the war she sees herself as fighting. Thus, she becomes engaged to Maynard Walker, whom she despises, because she believes he will be easy to manipulate in the interests of the cause, and after his death, she regularly visits Lockless playing the part of the grieving fiancée to manipulate Howell in the same way. She takes an interest in Hiram because she believes that he has the power of Conduction and knows how valuable that would be as a means of moving slaves to the North and freedom. To this end, she causes him much unnecessary suffering. The way that Corrine dictates to and exploits people is at times dangerously close to the ways in which the slave owners act, but she is highly intelligent and makes a series of ingenious and daring decisions that build the power and effectiveness of the Virginia Underground. For example, in order to protect Sophia, she arranges to buy her from Nathaniel, and before Howell dies, she arranges to settle his debts on the understanding that she will inherit Lockless. When she does, Corrine transforms it into another secret station and puts Hiram in charge.

Hawkins plays the role of Corrine's personal servant but is an Underground agent at the Bryceton station. He and his sister, **Amy**, were slaves at Bryceton in the time of Edmund Quinn, of whom he says, "'[he was] the meanest white man this world has known … Many years I watched him pose as a man of God toasting at the socials, sending his money to the alms-houses, money made off our backs'" (388). In some unspecified way, Corrine got rid of Edmund, took control of the estate, and secretly freed the slaves. For this Hawkins and Amy are grateful and work loyally under Corrine in the was on slavery. That said, even Hawkins sometimes admits that Corinne is so focused on the cause that she forgets the human aspect.

Micajah Bland, a white Underground agent who is part of Corrine Quinn's network, infiltrates Lockless as Maynard's tutor using the name Mr. Fields. Once Bland sees Hiram's intelligence, he offers to tutor him as well, teaching Hiram to read and write (a skill enslaved people were usually banned from acquiring) with the secret aim of recruiting Hiram as an Underground agent. After Hiram joins the Virginia Underground at Bryceton, he discovers the truth about his old tutor's role as an agent. The two travel together to the station in Philadelphia where Bland reveals his real name. Hiram and Bland develop a deep friendship which is cemented when he saves Hiram's life after he is kidnapped by slave-takers in Philadelphia. Bland volunteers to go to Alabama to conduct Otha White's wife Lydia and their two children out of slavery. In this he is initially successful, but during the journey back to Philadelphia, Lydia and the children are captured. Bland, who could just leave them to their fate, refuses to do so. As a result, he is taken and brutally murdered. Later in the narrative, we learn that it was Bland who sparked in Corrine her passionate hatred of the institution of slavery.

A Study Guide

Members of the Philadelphia Underground Railroad:

Harriet Tubman, a character based on the historical figure, is a legendary agent of the Underground Railroad known variously as The General, The Night, The Vanisher and Moses of the Shore. Harriet is unique in being the only Underground agent never to fail in a rescue attempt. She is from Maryland, where her free parents, Ma Rit and Pop Ross, and most of her siblings still live. Born into slavery, Harriet was inspired by a childhood friend named Abe to run and seek freedom in the North. Hiram accompanies her on a successful mission to liberate Harriet's brothers Ben, Henry, and Robert, as well as Henry's wife Jane. In the novel, Harriet also possesses the power of Conduction which enables her to travel large distances almost instantly. It is she who, during their time together, gives Hiram the understanding of the process that he needs in order to be able to control his own power.

Viola White is an escaped slave who lives in Philadelphia. She is the mother of Raymond and Otha.

Raymond White is an Underground agent in Philadelphia. He was born into slavery, but when he was a child his mother escaped to freedom with him, and they ended up living in Philadelphia. As a result, Raymond was separated from his brother, Otha, but subsequently Otha was able to buy his freedom and was reunited (largely by chance) with his family in Philadelphia. The two work as agents of the Underground together. Otha lives just outside the city with his parents.

Lambert White was left behind in slavery with Otha, who tells Hiram, "'Lambert died down there, far from home, far from the mother that birthed him and the father that reared him'" (210).

Otha White, Raymond's brother, was also born into slavery. When Otha was a child, his mother, Viola, fled with both him and his brother, Lambert. However, she and the boys were captured and re-enslaved. By the time she made her second attempt, she had to leave both Otha (about six) and Lambert (about eight) behind because at that point she had two younger children and literally could not carry them all. For a long time, Otha resented his mother for abandoning him and Lambert, but after he reunited with Viola, Raymond, and the rest of his family, he forgave her.

Lydia White, Otha's wife, remains a slave in Alabama with their three children, two girls and one boy. For years he has suffered terribly from the thought that he had to leave her there, and so he is overjoyed when Bland plans to go to Alabama and bring them all to safety. The rescue, however, fails and the fate of Lydia and her children is unresolved at the end of the novel.

Other Characters in Philadelphia:

Mars is a baker whom Hiram meets in Philadelphia. The first time he meets Hiram he tells him, "'Raymond and Otha – they both my cousin – blood of my dear

14

Hannah – and you with them, so that make you family to me'" (193). It is he, above all others, who teaches Hiram the true meaning of the word 'family'.

Hannah, Mars's wife, also works in the bakery.

Laura Bland is Micajah's sister whom Hiram meets in Philadelphia. It is never clear whether she is active in the Underground or whether she knows that her brother is an agent, and she just seems to disappear from the narrative following her brother's murder.

Mary Bronson is an enslaved woman brought north to Philadelphia by her master whom Raymond and Otha White and Hiram liberate together with her young son, **Octavius**.

Genre

Genre is defined as the class or category into which a work of art can be placed by its content, forms, technique, etc. Popular novel genres include: romance, science fiction, westerns, crime mysteries, and historical novels.

Bildungsroman or Coming of Age Novel

A *Bildungsroman* tells the story (often, though not exclusively, in the first person) of the growing up of a young, intelligent, and sensitive person who goes in search of answers to life's questions (including the biggest question: who they actually *are*) by gaining experience of the adult world from which they have been hitherto protected by their youth. The novel tells the story of the protagonist's adventures in the world and of the inner, psychological turmoil in his/her growth and development as a human being. Examples include: *Jane Eyre: An Autobiography* (1847) by Charlotte Brontë, *Great Expectations* (1861) and *David Copperfield* (1850) by Charles Dickens, *Sons and Lovers* (1913) by D. H. Lawrence, *A Portrait of the Artist as a Young Man* (1916) by James Joyce, *The Catcher in the Rye* (1951) by J. D. Salinger.

It is clear that *The Water Dancer* falls into this category. Its protagonist, Hiram Walker begins with a highly romanticized, indeed childish, view of the separation of Quality and Tasked. He learns the hard lesson that there is no way for a black person to bridge the gulf between the two, no matter how talented, intelligent and skillful that black person may be. He begins with the naïve view that it is blood that unites people into families, but he learns that Thena, his surrogate mother, is more his family than his biological farther, Howell Walker. Above all, he has to learn that in a marriage the man does not possess the woman; marriage is a union of two equal persons which does not take away the freedom and individualism of either. Coates has talked about the growth to consciousness of his protagonist:

> One of the challenges I faced is I felt like Hiram needed to be this 19th-century dude, so that meant 19th-century attitudes about gender. Because he was the protagonist of the story ... he has to struggle with how he feels about Sophia in the book. I think the struggle is probably a lot clearer [now] than it was in earlier drafts. Hiram wants individual freedom. And the book is about the recognition, from my perspective, that individual freedom is actually tied to all these other freedoms. So he can't actually be free, or have his freedom the way he wants it, and [treat Sophia like property]. That's not gonna work. I mean, she tells him that, first of all. She's very clear about it. He has a series of experiences where—it starts with him almost going to be like his [white] father. He wants to literally be like a white man, that's what he's thinking, and then comes to realize how corrupt that actually is, and what that means. (Coates interviewed by Hannah Giorgis)

16

The Water Dancer by Ta-Nehisi Coates

Magical Realism

Magic, or magical, realism is a term first used in the 1955 essay, "Magical Realism in Spanish American Fiction" by the critic Angel Floresto to describe narratives in which magical or supernatural events occur in an otherwise real-world setting and are described in the same matter-of-fact way. The novels of Gabriel García Márquez, particularly *One Hundred Years of Solitude* (1967), are most often seen as exemplifying the genre.

In *The Water Dancer*, the power of Conduction is presented as something real. Certainly, it can also be interpreted as a metaphor for liberation through memory, but characters in the novel actually do teleport over hundreds of miles. Coates has talked of his fascination from childhood with comic book heroes with super powers, so his inclusion of paranormal travel is hardly surprising. How well it works is an entirely different matter. Luke Murphy explains his reservations:

> [A]s promising as the idea of magic is, and the attached metaphor of Hiram not being able to come into the extent of his power until he accepts his history, it is at times a clunky, unwieldy presence in the book. The few times the novel does veer off the train tracks, losing its footing tonally, is when magic comes into play. That is not to say it doesn't work at all, for it often does, but the presence of literal magic does not work with the consistency of the story of Hiram and Sophia or Hiram and his relationships with people in the Underground.

The Novel of Ideas

Novels of ideas are fictions in which authors use situations and characters to examine, exemplify and/or critique abstract ideas in which they are interested. In such novels, the story expounds or explores a particular philosophical perspective on the world. Examples include: *The Time Machine* (1893) by H. G. Wells, *Nineteen Eighty-Four* (1949) and *Animal Farm* (1945) by George Orwell, and *The Handmaid's Tale* (1985) by Margaret Atwood. One inherent problem with the novel of ideas is that the ideas tend to take primacy over the plotting and the characters to the detriment of the novel as a work of literature. Anyone who has guiltily skipped over the dense pages of political philosophy and linguistics in *Nineteen Eighty-Four* to find out what happens to the rebels Winston and Julia will know exactly what I mean.

Once again, *The Water Dancer* self-evidently falls within this genre. Coates wants to educate the reader about slavery, specifically about what unfreedom *does* to people. In this way the novel is entirely consistent with his non-fiction writing, but it is an open question whether it works as a novel. Constance Grady is not alone in thinking that the urge to inform and educate sometimes triumphs over the creation of character and plot:

> *The Water Dancer* is a novel in which everyone talks in basically the same way, which means everyone talks in essays. And that, in

turn, means it is nearly impossible to get a real feel for any of the characters besides Hiram, because all of them are more or less interchangeable: They're just walking illustrations of various intellectual ideas that Coates would like to parse out.

In *The Water Dancer*, there is nothing to break up that monotony. The middle section of the book, in which Hiram meets a series of former Tasked people who are now working in the Underground, is honestly just a series of monologues. Every few pages the plot will stop cold while each new character delivers a speech explaining why slavery is an untenable evil, with examples pulled from their own lives. And then everyone else will agree with them and then we'll meet a new character who will shortly get their own monologue.

Wamuwi Mbao has the same criticism, "When yet another character is invoked to announce (and denounce) the evils of slavery, you begin to drum your fingers and wonder when the action is going to resume."

Historical Novel / Slave Narrative

The term historical novel applies to works set in a period at least twenty-five years before composition (e.g., a work such as Fenimore Cooper's *The Last of the Mohicans* which is set in 1757 and was written in 1826). Coates has spoken about the extensive research that he did in order to get not only the facts of slavery but more importantly the experience of enslavement right. Reviewers like Joan Gaylord are generally unanimous in pointing to the success of the narrative as historical fiction:

> With his exquisite writing, Coates delivers an adventure tale steeped in American history. The book imparts the experiences and motivations of the conductors on the Underground Railroad, and of those who supported their efforts – both in the North and the South. Coates weaves into the story references to the depletion of Virginia's soil caused by growing tobacco, which led to the demise of many Southern plantations, even as the owners fought desperately to retain their way of life. Hewing close to these historical facts brings an authenticity to the story.

Angela Ajayi concurs:

> No doubt, Coates – a former journalist for the *Atlantic* – has done his research. In a gorgeous, realist style reminiscent of the masters of 19th-century French literature, he captures with plodding detail and observation the grave, immoral world of slavery and the undeniable courage of those, including Harriet Tubman, who dared to protest it.

Slave narratives which give an account of the life of a former slave, either written or orally related by the slave, may either be based on the actual experiences of the narrator (in which case they are a sub-genre of autobiography or memoir) or fictional (in which case they are a sub-genre of the historical novel). Most real-life slave narratives were written between the mid-1700s and the late 1800s by African slaves in America. Neo-slave narratives, giving a fictional account of the slavery period from the first-person perspective, became popular in the last four decades of the twentieth century. Examples include: *Beloved* (1987) by Toni Morrison and *True North* (1996) by Kathryn Laski. For younger readers there is *The Seeds of America Trilogy*: *Chains* (2008), *Forge* (2010) and *Ashes* (2016) by Laurie Halse Anderson. Probably the most famous book in this genre is *Uncle Tom's Cabin* (1852) by Harriet Beecher Stowe – a fictionalized account of slavery that is much more hard-hitting than its reputation would lead readers to believe.

Settings and Structure

This isn't a typical first novel, if by "typical first novel" we mean a minor-chord and semi-autobiographical nibbling expedition around the margins of a life. *The Water Dancer* is a jeroboam of a book, a crowd-pleasing exercise in breakneck and often occult storytelling ... A lot happens in *The Water Dancer*. There are love stories. There are intimate betrayals. Hiram, on the lam or on missions for the Underground Railroad, is captured more than once. He gets to Philadelphia and experiences life as a free man. (Dwight Garner)

The one incident in the novel that, being based upon an actual event, can be dated with certainty is the escape from Maryland of Robert, Ben and Henry Tubman with the help of their sister Harriet, which happened on Christmas Day, 1854. At this time, Hiram Walker is around twenty years of age which places his birth c.1834.

The initial setting of the novel is Old Virginia, that is, the area in which large tobacco plantations were founded in the later seventeenth and eighteenth centuries. Tobacco, like cotton, is a labor-intensive crop and by the second half of the seventeenth century the institution of slavery, depending on the forced importation of black people from Africa, was well established in Virginia. As a crop, tobacco rapidly drains the soil of key nutrients. The solution to this problem requires the extensive fertilization of fields with animal manure or for 'old fields' to remain unplanted (fallow) for between ten and twenty years to restore the fertility of the soil (which accounts for the vast size of tobacco plantations). In a land which seemed to offer an inexhaustible supply of fertile, virgin land in the West, there was little incentive to preserve the fertility of the soil.

Hiram's first two decades coincide with the general exhaustion of the soil in Elm County; the once rich, red soil has turned to sand. (The same thing happened in the Dust Bowl areas of Oklahoma, Kansas, and northern Texas in the early 1930s.) Tobacco yields fall and therefore the income of the plantation owners declines significantly. This has two major consequences. First, many of the Quality simply move West, particularly into Tennessee and Kentucky, where the land will bring high tobacco yields. Thus, the aristocratic society of the traditional plantation families rather quickly disappears and a general economic decline sets in that affects all classes. Second, those planation owners who decide to hang on have to make up the economic shortfall due to falling tobacco income. The obvious way to do this is to sell the one thing of value that they have, their slaves. Thus, plantations like Lockless are caught in a vicious circle of decline: Howell continues planting tobacco in soil that annually produces less tobacco and tobacco of lower quality, and with fewer hands to work the plantation, both the farming side and the household side fall increasingly into decay.

The Water Dancer by Ta-Nehisi Coates

The other important setting of the narrative is Philadelphia, Pennsylvania, where Hiram lives for several months in 1854. The institution of slavery began in the Pennsylvania colony in 1684 when the slave ship *Isabella*, from Bristol, England, anchored in Philadelphia with 150 captured Africans. In the 1760s, nearly 4,500 enslaved blacks labored in Pennsylvania, and about one of every six white households in Philadelphia held at least one black person in bondage (Michael Coard). In 1780, Pennsylvania followed Vermont's abolition of slavery passing the first state Abolition Act in the United States. This ended slavery through gradual emancipation, and by the turn of the nineteenth century, there was an established African-American community in Pennsylvania. In August 1837, the Vigilant Association of Philadelphia, an abolitionist organization, was founded in Philadelphia to "create a fund to aid colored persons in distress." By 1850, the African-American William Still (1821-1902), a leading figure in Philadelphia's African-American community, was working with the Philadelphia Underground Railroad. He is credited with aiding as many as 800 slaves to escape to freedom. Like Raymond White in the novel, Still personally interviewed every freed person, keeping "careful records, including a brief biography and the destination for each, along with any alias adopted" (Wikipedia).

The city that Hiram experiences is different in almost every way from the world of Lockless and Starfall. He exchanges the Virginia countryside for a large, bustling, and frankly smelly, city. Since he is not there during the winter months, he does not have to deal with the intense cold, but he is surprised to find that in the height of summer the heat in the city is more intense and oppressive than that of summer in Virginia. Of course, he does not find Philadelphia to be a place where blacks and whites are equal: it is very quickly clear to him that the balance of power and wealth rests firmly with the whites. However, he is amazed to see that there *are* rich black – men and women dressed much more elegantly and expensively than the Virginia Quality. Then again, Philadelphia is not an entirely safe place for black people since they are always in danger of being abducted and taken South by slavers, but blacks do have legal rights and protections there which they are not allowed in Virginia.

The novel begins with the accident on the bridge without giving the reader any prior information about the main actors in the incident. These we are left to piece together from the narrative until Hiram fills in the back story by taking us back to the sale of his mother when he was nine. His travels with Maynard allow him to describe the local town of Starfall. However, having spent the first twenty years of his life in one small area of Virginia, following his failed attempt to escape he travels very widely in the next twelve months: Ryland's Jail, Bryceton Plantation, Philadelphia, up-state New York, Maryland, and back to Lockless. The protagonist's travels give the narrative a disjointed feel, as though the author is trying to cram all of the points he needs to hit into a very short period of time because the novel is one in which the protagonist's journey is a life-changing experience.

Narrative Voice

Two questions must necessarily be asked of *any* first-person narrative. First: Does the reader *trust* that the narrator gives an accurate account of what happens and a reliable interpretation and evaluation of its significance? Second: Is the reader convinced that the author *intends* the reader to trust the narrator? Everything is fine provided that the answers to these questions are either *both* in the affirmative or *both* in the negative because each of these alternatives implies that the text has consistency and artistic integrity. Problems occur when one of the answers is affirmative and the other negative, because this implies a loss of artistic control by the author and a flawed work of art.

The novelist Ford Madox Ford is generally credited with inventing 'the unreliable narrator' in *The Good Soldier* (1915) where John Dowell, introduces himself as a naïve witness to events which he proclaims himself to be constitutionally incapable of understanding because the passions, deceptions, hypocrisies and betrayals of those involved in the sad story he tells are beyond his power to comprehend. Thus, he opens his narrative with an open admission of his inability to draw a moral lesson:

> I don't know. And there is nothing to guide us. And if everything
> is so nebulous about a matter so elementary as the morals of sex,
> what is there to guide us in the more subtle morality of all other
> personal contacts, associations, and activities? Or are we meant to
> act on impulse alone? It is all a darkness.

What is distinctively original about John Dowell, however, is not that he *is* an unreliable narrator (Sterne's eponymous mid-eighteenth century narrator Tristram Shandy is that, if only because he is constitutionally incapable of sticking to the point), but that he *knows and declares himself to be so.*

In the case of *The Water Dancer*, the narrator is the mature Hiram looking back. He writes nostalgically, "Oh, to be back there, and be young again. To be seated in the dawning hours of my life, the sun of everything breaking over the horizon, and all the promises and tragedies ahead of me" (363). This suggests a perspective of several decades. Ron Charles writes that "Hiram narrates this story from a distance of many years, but he describes everything with bracing immediacy." Thus, the narrative not only describes the developing understanding of Hiram the young protagonist, but also embodies the developed understanding of Hiram the mature narrator. Nowhere is this more evident than in Hiram's attitude to Corrine Quinn, of whom the protagonist is often bitterly critical but of whom the narrator writes, "the less said about our remaining interview the better, for I hold her, all these years later, in the highest respect" (373). In producing his narrative, Hiram becomes the historian and archivist of his rediscovered family history.

To summarize, the mature Hiram Walker is an honest narrator whom the reader feels disposed to trust. As a young man he makes many errors of judgment about his place in the world, other people with whom he comes into contact, and events. As narrator, Hiram both conveys what he felt at the time and how he now regards those feelings. The one qualification may be with regard to Conduction. The reader suspects that even the mature narrator finds Conduction to be ultimately mysterious.

Themes

> The elevation of being white was not achieved through wine tastings and ice cream socials, but rather through the pillaging of life, liberty, labor and land; through the flaying of backs; the chaining of limbs; the strangling of dissidents; the destructions of families ... and various other acts meant ... to deny you and me the right to secure and govern our bodies.
>
> (Coates *Between the World and Me* quoted by Angela Ajayi)

The Meaning of Family

> I felt like we had this picture of enslavement that focuses on the physical and the visceral—on torture, on the rape, and the physical work. And all of that is there. That's actually in the book, but to me, as you point out, probably the most terrible aspect was the aspect of family separation. Of selling kids off for profit. Selling people's parents off for profit ... When I would read primary sources, that's what people talked about a lot. They talked about their relatives being sold off. I wanted folks to remember that this just wasn't a physical horror. It broke families. For money.
>
> (Coates in an interview with Hannah Giorgis)

Family and traditional familial values have long been a very important aspect of American culture – the idiom 'motherhood and apple pie' dates from World War II. The belief among political and Christian conservatives that the two-parent, heterosexual nuclear family unit, with a male breadwinner and female homemaker, was under attack was first reflected in the Republican Party platform of 1976. The Moral Majority, a political organization founded in 1979 by Baptist minister Jerry Falwell Sr., articulated the deeply held fear of many that "the social and political changes of the previous decade were altering traditional gender roles, loosening sexual norms, and weakening moral opposition to evils like homosexuality and pornography" (Neil Young "'Family Values' Conservatism Is Over"). At the same time, the undoubted problems of poverty, gangs, violence and drugs in the African American community is often seen as the result of the breakdown of the black family. Fox News host Bill O'Reilly is representative of many on the political Right when he states, "The reason there is so much violence and chaos in the black precincts is the disintegration of the African-American family. White people don't force black people to have babies out of wedlock." To state what is, I hope, obvious, Ta-Nehisi Coates is not on the political Right. In his *Atlantic* article, "The Black Family in the Age of Mass Incarceration" (Oct. 2015), he argues that there is a line of continuity that links slavery to the mass incarceration of young black men in contemporary America. In support of his thesis, Coates quotes President Lynden Johnson responding to the Moynihan Report at Howard University in June 1965. Highlighting "the breakdown of the Negro family structure," Johnson concluded, "For this, most of all, white America must accept responsibility … [because family breakdown] flows from centuries of oppression and persecution of the Negro man. It flows from the long years of degradation and discrimination, which have attacked his dignity and assaulted his ability to produce for his family."

Given Coates's position in the on-going debate into family values (summarized very briefly but, I hope fairly, above), it will not surprise the reader that *The Water Dancer* depicts in great detail the ways that slavery destroys the biological extended family units of the Tasked. The first, and most obvious, way in which this is seen to happen is the physical separation of family members. Initially this occurs when Africans are captured by or traded to slavers to be shipped in chains across the Atlantic; it continues when they are brought to the block and sold off, frequently with no regard for blood ties; and in Old Virginia, it accelerates when economic hardship motivates plantation owners to realize the capital that they have tied up in each person they hold enslaved. Most of the Tasked characters in the novel have had family members who have been sold Natchez-way or they have themselves been sold away from their blood relatives, and these separations are permanent. To give just two examples, when they were sold by Howell, Hiram lost both his mother, Rose, and his aunt, Emma, and when she was bought by Nathaniel Walker, Sophia lost her husband Mercury. Hiram's most valued memories are of Rose and his aunt Emma water dancing together and of his mother telling him stories about Africa at night.

There is, however, another form of separation that is perhaps even more destructive to the coherence of the black family unit. Attractive young black women are frequently subject to rape by white men, creating blood relations between the Quality and the Tasked which are not recognized in law. Thus, in terms of biology (blood), Hiram is the son of his white father Howell, Carrie is the daughter of Nathaniel, and Mary's child (assuming that she has one) is fathered by the son of her owner, Broadus. In most cases, the biological father takes no responsibility for his child, leaving the husband of the slave mother to take care of it which is something of a challenge. As Robert tells Hiram, "'I'd be damned if I was gon be raising some white man's child'" (292). At that point, Hiram finds it easy to offer advice on fatherhood, but he struggles to apply that same advice when he discovers that *his* Sophia has had a daughter by Nathaniel Walker. As he tells Sophia, the situation, "'Takes some adjusting [to]'" (348).

Arguably, the disruption to the family is even greater when, like Howell, the white father does take a role in the upbringing of his child because that role is circumscribed by the law regarding who is acceptable as white. It is not only that Hiram has to come to terms with the fact that the man to whom he looks up as his father and role model raped his mother and subsequently sold her, but he also has to deal with Howell's continued enslavement of him and forcing him to work as a manservant to his half-brother, Maynard. Even deeper than this, however, is the fact that Hiram, left with no blood family, desperately tries to become part of the Walker family, something that Thena warns him against when he is first called to work in the big house, "'They ain't your family, boy. I am more your mother standing right here now than that white man on that horse is your father,'" and something that the reader knows is impossible given the absolute division between the Quality and the Tasked in Virginia (22). Hiram makes the point that even the owners in these situations are damaged psychologically by the restrictions imposed by social norms: they have to keep their own children enslaved and are forced by economic pressures to sell them. Though the reader might not be disposed to feel much sympathy for him, in his old age, Howell evidently regrets many of the things that he has done, particularly to Rose and to Hiram. It is too easy for him to blame his actions on the pressures exerted by the racist norms of his time (the same pressures that Corrine Quinn has no difficulty in overcoming), but his regret and sadness are genuine.

The novel, however, does more than expose the many ways in which slavery destroys families: it also illustrates "the discernment needed to define family fluidly in the struggle created by the institution of slavery" (Shaun McMichael). Throughout the narrative, both enslaved and free black people who have been separated from their blood relations form new relationships of love and caring in the place of broken biological family ties. The most obvious example is Thena who becomes a surrogate mother to Hiram and, in doing so, both salves her own pain at the loss of all of her sold-away children and provides Hiram with a parent-sibling relationship that is much more real than the mirage of family that he has been pursuing with his biological father and his fantasies of being named Howell's heir. It takes Hiram a very long time to realize it, but he finally tells Thena, "'you … are all the family I have, more family than anyone who has ever lived in this house [i.e. Lockless]'" (326).

Mars is a baker whom Hiram meets in Philadelphia. Although he is in other ways a minor character, he has a tremendous influence in educating Hiram on the true, inclusive nature of the term 'family'. He tells Hiram when they first meet, "'Raymond and Otha – they both my cousin – blood of my dear Hannah – and you with them, so that make you family to me'" (193). The willingness of the Tasked to form ad hoc kinship networks with people outside their biological families is an entirely positive reaction to their tragic situation. They do so, however, in the full knowledge that these relationships are likely to be severed by separations in the near future, and they therefore see them as valuable but temporary. Otha, who is grieving his long-term separation from his wife and children, instructs Hiram, "'I lived divided from my blood, and made brothers wherever I lived, and grieved every time we were divided – and we were always divided. But I have never, for an instant, shied away from connection, from love.'" Remarkably, Otha's definition of family transcends not only biology but also race. Following the death of Micajah Bland in attempting to free Otha's wife and children, he tells Hiram, "'He was my brother, Hiram … Micajah Bland was not my blood, but he was so much my brother that he would die for me and mine'" (258).

The Water Dancer by Ta-Nehisi Coates

The Importance of Memory

But there is also this truth, one Coates has pursued his entire professional life: We cannot abandon our obligations to keep alive history that too many – from politicians to journalists to educators – have sought to suppress. If those who still suffer most from this nation's greatest sin, cease to bear witness to this high crime, if our ancestors cannot speak through our voices, then our silence becomes a convenient narrative for the masters. (Renée Graham)

In an NPR interview with Terry Gross, Coates says this of his fascination with memory, "For the past 10 years, in a lot of my writing, I've thought a lot about memory, and why certain things I remembered a certain kind of way. And I've thought quite a bit about the fact that much of the country's history is premised on forgetting, not remembering, certain things." This comment alerts readers to the two levels on which memory exists in *The Water Dancer*: the cultural and the personal.

Coates has long argued that in America slavery appears to generate collective amnesia. In the South, the historical reality of a war fought to preserve the right of whites to own blacks has been subsumed under the myth of Lost Cause in the fight for States' Rights. When people gather to protest against taking down statues of Civil War Confederate heroes (most of them erected decades after the end of that conflict), they are motivated by myth that has risen to the status of truth. Coates tells Jeffrey Brown, "I think part of the history of racism and white supremacy in this country is the – just the stranglehold it's had on the story the country tells itself" (*PBS News Hour Transcript*). In the novel, the Quality willfully turn a collective blind eye to the fact that their wealth and position, the very houses they occupy and the clothes they wear, have been gained over the blood and bone of those they have enslaved. Bill Capossere writes, "They have lost their past"; they have created "a society wholly unmoored from memory," and Wamuwi Mbao says, "the fine society of antebellum America is a rotten brocade woven from wilful [sic] self-deception." Yet Coates believes that failure to remember what happened in relation to slavery is as prevalent, and as serious in its consequences, amongst the African American community as it is amongst the dominant white community. In the same interview he says:

So, a lot of this is about how African-Americans remember their own history.

They are – and I think this is no longer true, but, certainly, let's say, two or three generations before me, there certainly was a prevailing notion that we didn't talk about enslavement. We just didn't mention it. You just move on. You don't repeat the traumas. But one of the implicit ideas, I think, in this is that you can't actually move. There's so much that you can't do when you're so intent on forgetting. And there's so much more you can do if you

27

actually grab it by the reins, you know, grab memories by the reins and say, look, this actually – this happened. (*PBS News Hour Transcript*)

To know who we are, we need to acknowledge from where we come. *The Water Dances*, then, is intended as a reality check – a jolt to the nation's collective memory.

In the novel, we see that the Tasked (i.e., enslaved people as a group) have been forcibly separated from their homeland of Africa and from their native languages, religions, customs and cultures so that, within a generation or two, individuals like Hiram have lost connection with their ancestors and so have no sense of their own identity. The water dance, for example, is continued but its symbolic significance related to Conduction by water has been lost to all but a few. One of the most obvious ways in which slaves were denied access to their past was through being kept illiterate. This is why Raymond White in Pennsylvania considers it so important to make a written record of the testimony of every person saved by the Underground.

We also see how slavery robs individuals of their memories of their personal history because those memories are just too painful to bear. Thus Hiram, who in other respects has a photographic memory, has involuntarily repressed almost every memory of his birth mother, and Thena, Hiram's surrogate mother, who has had all of her children sold down South, has blocked out even their existence. The only difference seems to be that Hiram's childhood consciousness has acted to block access to his memories, while the adult Thena has consciously sought to block out her memories. It is a distinction without a difference, however, for both are employing a necessary coping mechanism to deal with traumatic experiences. Thus, when Hiram tells Thena that he has found her daughter Kessiah and made a promise to reunite the two, she does not react with the joy he naïvely expects, but with anger and resentment generated by fear of reopening a psychic wound. She asks Hiram rhetorically, "Why you bring this back to me? Why you do this? ... I have settled up with it. Why you bring this to me? ... Do you know what it took for me to make peace with this? ... How dare you bring me back like this?" (383-384). Reflecting on Thena's reaction, Hiram comments, "I should not have been surprised. I knew by then how much the past weighs on us ... worst of all I knew how the memory of such things altered us, how we could never escape it, how it became an awful part of us" (384).

Nevertheless, Thena does eventually embrace her past, and only by so doing is she able, to some extent, to free herself of the wound the loss of her children has created. The same may be said of Hiram, who finally recovers the memory of his mother's escape attempt and of Howell's vindictive sale of her, but in Hiram's case this liberation results in the ability to control his power of Conduction which becomes a tool he uses to convey himself and others to freedom. Memories, even when they are painful, are empowering; they are an essential element of the struggle for freedom in both the individual and the group. Harriet instructs Hiram,

The Water Dancer by Ta-Nehisi Coates

"'We forget nothing, you and I … To forget is to truly slave. To forget is to die … For memory is the chariot, and memory is the way, and memory is bridge from the curse of slavery to the boon of freedom'" (271). This is the rationale behind the operation of Conduction. The jump is made by the power of remembered stories; these destroy both distance and time, and by their power they enable the corporate body to do likewise.

Though readers may differ on how effective this magic element is, as a metaphor for the way that slavery is so often erased from the American public consciousness it is very powerful. Constance Grady writes:

> The hole in Hiram's memory where his mother used to be forms the central metaphor of *The Water Dancer*. Coates has long argued that one of America's great sins is not just slavery, but our refusal to look the fact of slavery in the face, to grapple honestly with the fact that slavery was foundational to our country and that its aftereffects are still with us. That's why Hiram must allow himself to fully experience the worst thing that slavery brought upon him – the ripping away of his mother – in order to come fully into his powers. It's a rich, intellectually interesting metaphor, if nowhere near as elegantly deployed as the similar metaphor in *Beloved* that Coates is cribbing from. (It's a high bar!)

Coates argues that as a society the true transition from slavery to freedom is only possible by fully reckoning with the past. The connection between Hiram's forgetting of the traumas in his own life and the cultural erasure of enslaved people's African heritage is made clear when one of the details about his mother that Hiram finally remembers is that she used to tell him stories about Africa at night.

The Skills of the Enslaved

> Slaves had many noteworthy skills and talents which made plantations economically self-sufficient. The services of slave blacksmiths, carpenters, coopers, shoemakers, tanners, spinners, weavers and other artisans were all used to keep plantations running smoothly, efficiently, and with little added expense to the owners. These same abilities were also used to improve conditions in the quarters so that slaves developed not only a spirit of self-reliance but experienced a measure of autonomy. These skills, when added to other talents for cooking, quilting, weaving, medicine, music, song, dance, and storytelling, instilled in slaves the sense that, as a group, they were not only competent but gifted. ("The Cultural Landscape of the Plantation: Slave Skills and Talents")

Slavery is, by definition, a system of stolen labor, but the stereotype many people have of the slave is of a man or woman forced by the whip to engage in

29

hour after hour of back-breaking manual work in the tobacco, cotton or sugar fields. In *The Water Dancer*, however, Coates presents the Tasked as skilled, knowledgeable, and competent – more so, indeed, than their so-called masters. Aside from endowing two characters (Hiram and Harriet) with superpowers which derive from their African roots, Coates shows virtually every one of his enslaved characters as possessing extraordinary abilities: both Big John and Georgie Parks are experts in soil cultivation; Ella is something of a gourmet cook; Mars and his wife Hanna run a successful bakery; Hiram himself has a photographic memory and a first-rate intelligence. Not only are these skills appropriated by the slave owners, but they are often stifled because the Tasked are not allowed any opportunities to use the skills they have.

Coates reverses the stereotype of black people as inherently lazy, child-like and lacking intelligence which was often used as a justification for slavery, as Confederate Vice President Alexander H. Stephens did when speaking at the Athenaeum in Savannah, Georgia, on March 21st, 1861:

> The new constitution has put at rest, forever, all the agitating questions relating to our peculiar institution, African slavery as it exists amongst us – the proper status of the negro in our form of civilization. ... The prevailing ideas entertained by him [Thomas Jefferson] and most of the leading statesmen at the time of the formation of the old constitution, were that the enslavement of the African was in violation of the laws of nature; that it was wrong in principle, socially, morally, and politically ... Our new government is founded upon exactly the opposite ideas; its foundations are laid, its cornerstone rests, upon the great truth that the negro is not equal to the white man; that slavery, subordination to the superior race, is his natural and normal condition. This, our new government, is the first, in the history of the world, based upon this great physical, philosophical, and moral truth.

In opposition to this view, Coates shows the enslaved to be more capable than their enslavers. What Hiram says of his half-brother is true of the Quality in general, "slavery made a child of him" (7). He further explains, "The masters could not bring water to boil, harness a horse, nor strap their own drawers without us. We were better than them – we had to be. Sloth was literal death for us, while for them it was the whole ambition of their lives" (35).

The novel charts a decline in the landowning whites from their intrepid and ingenious ancestors who founded the great plantations, literally hacking them out of the virgin earth, and built the great mansions from scratch, to the current generation watching impotently as each crop of tobacco robs the soil of its last remaining nutrients, and it locates the cause of the decline on the complete dependence of the masters on the labor of enslaved people. The point is made most clearly in the stark contrast between the intelligent and gifted Hiram and his lazy, incapable, uneducated half-brother, Maynard. White people like Maynard only maintained their position of superiority on the back of the skills, power, and knowledge of those they enslaved, but by doing so they further sap their own abilities.

Hiram is caught in the same trap as many of the other Tasked: his intelligence and skills will never allow him to rise in Virginia society, they simply make him a more valuable asset to his owner. Hiram reflects, "I knew I would never advance beyond my blood-bound place at Lockless. And I knew by now that my genius would not save me, indeed my genius would only make me a more valuable commodity" (108). The irony of the novel's conclusion is that, while through his own skills and courage (and, of course, his magical super power) he does effectively become the master of Lockless when it becomes a station of the Underground Railroad, all of this has to be kept secret.

It is not, however, only in the realm of academic, practical or artisanal skills that the Tasked are shown to have abilities denied to their white masters. They are presented as the natural inheritors of a rich and mystical African culture. Ironically it is Corrine, a convert to the cause, who pays tribute to what she sees as the superior wisdom of the Tasked telling Hiram, "'I am convinced that the most degraded field-hand … knew more of the world than any overstuffed, forth-holding American philosophe … the dance and song of your people … is an unwritten library stuffed with a knowledge of this tragic world, such that it defies language itself. Power makes slaves of masters, for it cuts them away from the world they claim to comprehend'" (153). Conduction is established as a natural part of that inheritance though one which, like so many other skills, is slowly being lost. Harriet tells Hiram, "'It was a known practice among the older ones … But we are here now. And we have forgotten the old songs and lost so many of our stories'" (280). Perhaps Hiram will prove to be its last exponent.

The Liberating Medium of Water

For Africans, slavery began with the Middle Passage, that journey across the Atlantic Ocean that enslaved blacks made chained together in the holds of slave ships and with the collective trauma which resulted. This trade was ended in 1808 following the passage of The Act Prohibiting Importation of Slaves of 1807 that banned the importation of slaves into the United States. This law did not seek to restrict the domestic slave trade; in fact, with the legal supply of imported slaves terminated, the domestic trade increased in importance and slaves became a more valuable commodity. Thus, to the Tasked of Elm County there remains a further threat that links water with loss of freedom, that of being sold in Natchez and forcible transported down the River Mississippi to the cotton plantations of the Deep South. However, the novel also shows that water is the medium by which slaves may regain their freedom. This is illustrated on the purely realistic level by the case of Mary Bronson and her young son Octavius, two slaves who are brought north to Philadelphia by riverboat on the Delaware and there achieve their freedom through the intervention of the Underground. Nevertheless, it remains true that the main thrust of the novel is to show the mystical connection between water and emancipation.

This connection is symbolized by the water dance, in which a woman moves rhythmically while balancing a jar full of water on their head without spilling any of the contents. Throughout the novel, dance is depicted as a concrete expression of freedom since it involves a control of one's own body which is the very antithesis of the ownership of that body by another human being. At the Christmas celebration, Hiram describes, "everyone in the Street dancing ... It was an entire nation in movement." In particular, he notices Sophia doing the water dance, "I watched Sophia, a flurry of limbs, but all under control, and the jar seemingly fused to her head" (93). The dance is thus inherently an act of rebellion: participants in the dance have full control (i.e., ownership) of their bodies. As Indiana Seresin comments, "The phrase 'under control' illustrates that for Sophia, dancing is a reminder (to herself and others) of her ownership of her own body." In his final act of Conduction, Hiram summons up the memory of slaves from Lockless being sold in great numbers following the fall in tobacco revenues:

> And now, where the phantoms had once danced before us, we
> saw ... these same men and women ... where they had once
> worn looks of great joy, there was now sorrow ... where their
> arms and their legs had once been dancing, I saw now that from
> ankle to wrist they were chained. (395)

The water dance is more, however, than either a merely symbolic expression or a minor, inconsequential physical expression of freedom; it is intimately related to the magical power of Conduction that was once, in the old times, part of the birthright of all Africans. Harriet gets Hiram to trust himself to the water by comparing Conduction to dancing, "'Stay with me, friend ... No exertions needed. It's just like dancing. Stay with the sound, stay with the story and you will be fine'" (271). Following their first experience of Conduction together, Hiram repeats the same reassurance to Sophia, telling her that moving across the river is "'like dancing'" (378), and Sophia explains the full significance of the water dance. Sophia tells Hiram:

> "Was a big king who come over from Africa on the slave ship with
> his people. But when they got close to shore, him and his folk took
> over, killed all the white folks, threw 'em overboard, and tried to
> sail back home. But the ship run aground, and when the king look
> out, he see that the white folks' army is coming for him with they
> guns and all. So the chief told his people to walk out into the water,
> to sing and dance as they walked, that the water-goddess brought
> 'em here, and the water-goddess would take 'em back home.
> "And when we dance as we do, with the water balanced on our
> head, we are giving praise to them who danced on the waves. We
> have flipped it, you see?" (379).

Conduction flips the relationship of slaves to water in a magical but (the novel insists) very real and practical way. Just as the captives on the slave ship used the power of water to return them to their homeland, so right at the start of the novel that same power saves Hiram from drowning in the River Goose, for his memory of his mother performing the water dance provides a link to his ancestral power to use the water as a medium freedom. Later Harriet and Hiram teleport enslaved people to Free States.

[I should here acknowledge my debt in the section above to "Themes: Water, Movement, and Freedom" in LitCharts by Indiana Seresin.]

The Corrosive Effects of Slavery

[A] constant [in the novel] is pain; not just the hurt of a motherless boy whose white father cares for him only conditionally, pleased by his handiness and quick brain, but the much broader stain of slavery — the constant ache, he confides, "of being born into a world of forbidden victuals and tantalizing untouchables — the land around you, the clothes you hem, the biscuits you bake. You bury the longing, because you know where it must lead." (Leah Greenblatt)

We have already noted that *The Water Dancer* argues that slavery emasculates the predominantly male plantation owners in Virginia by providing them with an excuse for not exerting themselves at a time when the impoverishment of the soil requires that they should be proactive. Thus, slavery infantizes Maynard, both in Hiram's dreams and in reality, by making him helpless and totally reliant on his half-brother. Howell is scarcely any better than his legitimate son. His only solution to the cash crisis at Lockless is to sell his slaves (thus reducing his capital), to borrow (which results in Corrine inheriting the plantation) and to rely on Hiram (who is, of course, a slave). Slavery traps the white masters in a vicious circle of decline. Less is shown of the ladies of Quality, but enough to reveal them to be spoilt, pampered and petulant. With black maids to do everything for them, their lives are empty and without meaning.

Slavery does more than this, however, for the institution allows whites to give free reign to their meanest, most brutal instincts because they face no legal consequences. This brutalizing effect ranges from the Quality lady Alice Caulley slapping a black servant and demanding a song, to the Low whites who, night after night, hunt captured slaves for their own pleasure. At the same time, the system actively prevents characters from acting on their better impulses. Everything Howell says about this awareness of Hiram's abilities and his desire to show him favor rings true, yet he feels himself to be constrained by the written laws and unwritten rules of slavery only to do for Hiram things that society will find acceptable. Similarly, there is no reason to doubt that Georgie Parks (who, though black, is no longer a slave) genuinely likes and admires Hiram, and does everything he can to dissuade Hiram from trying to run. However, when Hiram shows himself to be quite determined, Georgie's position as a free black man in Starfall is so precarious that he simply cannot take the risk of aiding him: his only alternative is to betray Hiram.

Coates goes still further by suggesting that *some* white abolitionists (the ones Hiram terms "fanatical") act not out of love for the enslaved but out of selfish anger. He explains, "They took slavery as a personal insult or affront, a stain upon their name ... Slavery humiliated them, because it offended a basic sense of goodness that they believed themselves to possess ... So their opposition was a kind of vanity, a hatred of slavery that far outranked any love of the slave" (370-371). Just as Maynard may be said to epitomize the debilitating impact of owning slaves on the Quality, so Corrine Quinn encapsulates the dehumanizing effect of fighting slavery on some of the white members of the Underground. Some of the actions Corrine takes in her war on the institution are not approved of by other members of the Underground, particularly those in the North like the White brothers and Harriet Tubman. Hawkins identifies the problem when he explains to Hiram, "'We forget sometimes – it is freedom we are serving, it is the Task that we are against'" (390). Raymond White distances himself and the Philadelphia Underground from Corrine's methods:

> "I know well the methods and reputation of Corrine Quinn. They
> are not my methods, Hiram, no matter their aim ... This ritual
> burial, the hunting, the chasing, it is all abhorrent to me ... it was
> wrong ... to our cause ... no matter what power may beat in your
> breast." (220)

Micajah Bland, who during his time in Virginia followed Corrine's orders, explains, "'when you are operating as Corrine Quinn does, on the other side of the line, the math is different. It has to be. You were part of that math'" (221). To Corrine, Hiram is not a person but an abstraction, a chess piece to be sacrificed, if necessary, in the grand strategy to bring down slavery, but later Bland does not see the struggle this way and apologizes to Hiram for the suffering he put him through. Nor is Corrine alone. Bland himself, a thoroughly admirable character, allows his passions to rule his reason during a rescue and gets himself needlessly killed.

This is not to imply that the novel equates the slave-owning Quality with fanatical white abolitionists. Corrine Quinn takes immense risks and does a great deal of good. We can also say that Hiram and Corrine have a good influence on each other: Corrine teaches Hiram that fighting slavery is not just about helping the people for whom he cares. In turn, Hiram teaches Corrine that sometimes individual human beings are more important than an abstract cause, as when near the end of the novel she complains about his disobeying her orders not to conduct Thena:

> "I don't like it," said Corrine. "It is a problem. I must be able to
> depend on my agents. I have to know their minds."
> I shook my head and laughed. "Do you ever hear yourself?"
> She was silent for a moment and then smiles.
> "I do," she said. "I do. But I need reminding every now and

again." (401)

That she listens to him is reflected in his final verdict on her, "I hold her, all these years later, in the highest respect" (373).

In portraying the impact of slavery on black characters in the novel, Coates may be thought to have shown them to be too resilient. He has stated that he deliberately looked to portray the deep emotional and psychological impact of slavery rather than the more obvious, and very real, physical brutalities (though these are by no means absent from the novel). "Coates doesn't linger on the gruesome realities of slavery. There are no extended scenes of abuse," writes Dwight Garner. Thena is turned from a gregarious, child-loving woman into a mean scold; the old man Hiram meets in jail has been so robbed of his humanity that he seems only to want to die; Lydia and her children remain in slavery separated from her husband Otha … the examples of suffering are many. However, the warm humanity that Hiram finds in Philadelphia, while heartwarming, suggests that, once free, ex-slaves are able to put their suffering behind them and this is just not plausible.

The Need for Resistance

Arguably the most important theme in the novel is the need to keep fighting, not only against slavery but against all of those institutionalized prejudices that rob people of their right to equality. [We hold these truths to be self-evident, that all men are created equal, that they are endowed by their Creator with certain unalienable Rights, that among these are Life, Liberty and the pursuit of Happiness." The Declaration of Independence, 1776.] In reference to slavery, almost every possible reaction is presented and found to be wanting: some characters simply exploit the advantage the institution gives them with no thought to the victims (Nathaniel, Maynard, Alice Caulley, the Low in general); others try to work within the system to get what they want (Howell, Georgie Parks); some suffer in helpless despair (Thena, Ella, Lambert White); some are so fanatical in their hatred of slavery that they sometimes forget to love (Corrine, Bland). Each and every one of these characters fails. The only characters who succeed are those who fight slavery while retaining their humanity (Raymond and Otha White, Harriet Tubman). Ultimately, Hiram and Sophia join this group.

The point of the novel is not, however, to examine a historical situation but to prompt the reader to apply the lessons of Hiram's narrative to the present. This is made clear in the other issue that Hiram has to deal with (as though slavery were not enough!) which is the patriarchal and misogynistic nature of the pervading culture, as reflected, for example in Howell's rape of Rose, Maynard's treatment of prostitutes, and Nathaniel's weekly rape of Sophia. Hiram is slow to understand that to Sophia it makes no sense to escape being owned by a white master and then allow herself to be subject to a black husband. Elias Rodriques comments, "The novel's women play a central role in moving the narrative forward and in helping Hiram discover the ways that he must change to liberate himself and others." Here is an issue that no reader can consign to history. That is the point of Hiram's experience of the convention in up-state New York where he is exposed to a wide range of "[n]ew ways of being, new ideas of liberation" (245) – abolition of alcohol, equal rights for women, rights for native peoples, an end to child laborer, the right to unionize, communal living, and free love. Just as Hiram is forced to review things that he has taken for granted, so is the reader challenged to do the same. The novel is a call to action, particularly amongst the black community, because emancipation was only the beginning.

Symbolism

The comments in this section will be brief in order to avoid repetition.

Water Dancing

Water represents baptism, cleansing and rebirth. Water dancing is a symbolic cultural expression of control over water and therefore of freedom. It is an echo of the ancient African ability of Conduction, which is literally the building, through the operation of the imagination on memories and stories, of bridges over the water.

The Bridge Over the River Goose

The bridge from which Hiram falls represents the powerlessness of slavery. It is the bridge over which his mother Rose, in chains, was led away to be sold down the River Mississippi as hundreds of others had been and would continue to be.

Conduction

Teleportation in the novel is a (magical) real thing, but Conduction is also a symbol of freedom. Harriet and Hiram achieve Conduction only when they recover and reanimate their past memories and stories. It is a metaphor for the power that a person gets from knowing who they are, where they come from, and how they relate to the world.

The River Goose

River Goose is, for the Tasked, a symbol of hope and freedom because it is linked in their minds with the story of Hiram's grandmother, Santi Bess, leading forty-eight enslaved people to freedom by walking with them into its waters. This modern myth is connected in the minds of the Tasked with the stories of the Africans who jumped from slave ships and were transported back to their native land.

Lockless

Lockless is a symbol of the Virginia version of the institution of slavery (as distinct from the even more brutal and repressive version in the Deep South). Its name reflects the self-delusion of the founders of the plantation that the Tasked are not kept confined by locks, chains and corporal punishment because they are happy. To the Tasked, however, the name is ironic since escape is so difficult that such measures are not necessary. By the end of the novel, the name Lockless is ironic in a completely different way since, as a secret station of the Underground, it works to open the locks that keep slaves confined against their will.

The Coffin

'The coffin' is a phrase the Tasked use to describe slavery, particularly as it exists in the Deep South. Slavery literally takes away the lives of the enslaved: henceforth their lives (like their bodies) belong to their master: it is a living death.

The old man whom Hiram shares a prison cell says this about how he felt when, despite having promised his late wife that he would protect their son, that son was sold away, "'a man that can't honor his wife's dying wish ain't even a man, ain't even a life'" (132).

Guide to the Novel

PART ONE

Chapter I

Notes:

"the river Goose" (3): Goose River (or Creek) rises at Manassas Gap in the Blue Ridge Mountains. It runs for fifty-four miles before discharging into the Potomac River.

"turnpike" (3): i.e., a toll road. Goose Creek Bridge is on Ashby's Gap Turnpike.

"that direction was south" (3) – Conditions for slaves generally got much worse further into the Deep South. The expression 'sold down the river' dates from the mid-1800s and alludes to slaves being sold in somewhere like Natchez and transported down the Mississippi River to labor on cotton plantations.

"Natchez" (3): Slavery began in Natchez, Mississippi, in 1719 and continued through the periods of French, British, Spanish and American rule until it was ended in 1863, during the Civil War, when President Abraham Lincoln signed the Emancipation Proclamation. Known as the Forks of the Road, Natchez was, in the years before the Civil War, the second-largest slave market in the South.

"patting juba" (4): "Pattin' Juba . . is an African American style of dance that involves stomping as well as slapping and patting the arms, legs, chest, and cheeks (clapping) … The Juba dance was originally brought by Kongo slaves to Charleston, South Carolina. It became an African-American plantation dance that was performed by slaves during their gatherings when no rhythm instruments were allowed due to fear of secret codes hidden in the drumming." (Wikipedia contributors. "Juba dance." *Wikipedia, The Free Encyclopedia*. Wikipedia, The Free Encyclopedia. 9 Dec. 2019. Web. 18 Dec. 2019.)

"Millennium chaise" (4): A four-wheeled carriage with a closed cabin that could accommodate two or three passengers. The driver sat on the box in front in the open air.

"Starfall" (5): I have not found a town of this name.

"a fancy" (5): i.e., a fancy woman or prostitute.

"Dumb Silk Road" (5): I can find no source for this name.

"diorama" (6): i.e., a model representing a scene in three-dimensions.

"under the ox" (8): This sounds like an idiom, probably an old Southern or slave saying, that seems to mean 'as good as dead' or 'as good as in our grave."

Guiding Questions:

1. The narrator calls the bridge, "that fantastic bridge between the land of the living and the land of the lost" (4). Who are the "living"? Who are the "lost"?

2. What particular significance does this bridge have for the narrator who, as a result, has "always avoided" it (3)? Why could the vision he has of his mother dancing *only* have happened on *this* particular bridge?

3. About what is the narrator thinking immediately before the chaise he is driving plunges over the side of the bridge?

4. The narrator writes of Maynard, "I can now say that slavery murdered him" (7). Explain what he means.

5. Who is the boy in the "apparition" that the narrator sees in the final paragraph of the chapter just before, he assumes, he is going to drown? What is happening?

6. What is the significance of the necklace?

Summary:

The action involves an accident in which a carriage carrying three people (Hiram, the black narrator; Maynard, his white half-brother; and an unnamed prostitute) falls from a bridge into the River Goose. Maynard and Hiram, who seems to be more like Maynard's minder than his half-brother, are returning to Lockless from a race meeting where Maynard has won big on a bet. Shunned by the Virginia Quality, Maynard has insisted that Hiram take him to a whorehouse and is bringing a whore back home with them.

Distracted by a vision of his long-lost mother, Rose, water dancing, and wrapped up in thoughts about those slaves who have (like his mother) crossed this bridge to be sold south, Hiram drives off the road, plunging the carriage into the water. The woman is instantly swept away. Maynard, who cannot swim, calls to Hiram for help, but Hiram, who is convinced that he is about to die, cannot do anything to save him – though in truth he makes no real effort to do so.

The psychological action involving Hiram's feelings and memories is inseparable from the physical action. Approaching the bridge triggers a vision because this has to have been the bridge over which his "bound" mother passed when she was taken to Natchez to be sold (3). Hiram sees a vision of his mother, Rose, as she was in her youth, carrying a large jar on her head filled with water which, despite her dance-like movements, she does not spill. In retrospect, Hiram realizes that at that moment the stone bridge was not merely a way of linking the two river banks, but a "fantastic bridge between the land of the living and the land of the lost ... Legions of the lost, brought across that baleful bridge, legions embodied in my dancing mother" (4-5). This, in turn, triggers a memory of Rose dancing in a circle of his people (i.e., slaves) including Aunt Emma and Uncle John. Rose had been the best dancer at Lockless, which is what had attracted his father, the plantation owner, to her.

As he feels himself to be drowning, Hiram reports that something happens that "shook forever my sense of a cosmic order" (5). The repressed memories flood back. Hiram remembers Rose coming to say farewell to him the day before she was taken away. He also recalls being instructed by his father to protect his half-brother, but he now feels liberated from the constrains of slavery. Death will free Hiram from the chain by which Maynard holds him.

Analysis:

Without background or explanation, the novel jumps right into the action:

people, places and events are referred to by the narrator (we learn only that he is called "Hi") who, of course, is entirely familiar with all of these in a way that the reader is not. Moreover, the action into which we are precipitated is both physical and psychological; it encompasses the present and the past. Only in retrospect does the reader understand that this chapter introduces the novel's main themes.

There is a contrast between the nature of family amongst the Quality and the Tasked. While Hiram's father (the unnamed master of Lockless) has shown great concern to protect his legitimate, white son, Maynard, he has shown no such concern about Rose, the mother of his illegitimate, mixed-race son, Hiram, whom he sold south Natchez-way. Family separation is a reality of life amongst the Tasked, which means that black people like Hiram are only able to connect with lost family members through memory. However, in Hiram's case the sale of his mother has been so traumatic that his mind has repressed all recollection of her. The vision he has of Rose makes him realize, "how I had pushed my memory of her into the 'down there' of my mind, how I forgot, but did not forget" (3). What he understands at this moment of crisis is "the awesome power of memory" to liberate the individual from the confines of time and space. Hiram feels himself enveloped in a blue light and experiences, "peace ... [and] freedom ... [and he] knew that the elders had not lied, that there really was a homeplace of our own, a life beyond the Task" (8-9).

Feeling himself to be near death, Hiram frees himself from the weight of Maynard that is, both literally and figuratively, pulling him down. He recovers the memory of his last tender, terrible moments with his mother – the memory that was so traumatic that he repressed it. This recovered memory gives Hiram his first experience of Conduction, "[memory] can open a blue door from one world to another ... memory can fold the land like cloth" (3). Conduction will literally save his life.

The relationship between Hiram and his half-brother is a microcosm of the relationship between slaves and masters. Despite being brothers, the reality is that Maynard is Hiram's enslaver despite the other reality that Hiram is in every other way superior to Maynard. Hiram feels, "I could never, in this life, be free of him ... who held my chain" (5). As he is fighting for his life in the water, Hiram recalls the times he tried, and failed, to teach Maynard to swim. Maynard refused to apply himself in this as in everything else he did because Hiram would always be there to save him. Hiram reflects that Maynard became totally dependent on his slaves and incapable of acting independently. In the same way, although the subjugation of the Tasked is justified by the belief of whites that black people are inferior, it actually results in the Quality being deficient in the knowledge, application, and skills they need to prosper – even to survive. Hiram reflects about his half-brother, "slavery murdered him ... slavery made a child of him" (7). One indication of this general truth is that the Virginia earth that in Hiram's childhood was "still red as brick and red with life" (3) has become exhausted by monoculture. The Quality have seen this happening and done nothing to stop it.

Chapter II

Notes:
"Elm County" (11): There is an Elm Grove (aka the Williams-Rick House), a historic plantation house in Southampton County, Virginia, but there is no Elm County in Virginia.
"osnaburg" (11): i.e., a durable, coarsely woven cotton fabric.
"brogans" (12): i.e., coarse, stout leather shoes reaching to the ankle.
"the Street" (12): Historically called Slave Row, the place where the slaves' cabins were. Every plantation had one.
"rope bed" (13): i.e., a wooden frame strung with ropes to support a mattress.
"peck of corn" (14): A peck is a largely obsolete unit of dry volume, equivalent to two dry gallons. Corn husks are not measured in pecks, so this would be corn kernels (i.e., niblets).
"Tennessee Pacer" (20): Also called a Tennessee Walking Horse or Tennessee Walker, this is a breed of horse with a unique four-beat running-walk and flashy movement. "It is a popular riding horse due to its calm disposition, smooth gaits and sure-footedness." (Wikipedia contributors. "Tennessee Walking Horse." *Wikipedia, The Free Encyclopedia*. Wikipedia, The Free Encyclopedia. 18 Dec. 2019. Web. 19 Dec. 2019.)

Guiding Questions:
7. How would you explain that a boy with a photographic memory discovers the day after his mother left him that his recollections of her consist of "nothing but ephemera, shadows, and screams" (11)?
8. Looking into the water trough, the narrator feels the light pulling him into the trough. His is convinced that he has found "a secret path that would deliver me from Lockless to reunite with my mother" (13). What actually happens? Why does it happen now?
9. On the surface, Thena is the last person the narrator might choose to live with. Explain why. So why *does* he choose her?
10. What is "the precise root of [Thena's] rage" (15)? What does she mean when she says that there, "'wasn't nothing natural about'" her husband's death and that Big John "'was murdered'" (17)?
11. Explain why Thena is so insistent in telling Hiram, "'You cannot forget'" (18).
12. Hiram refers to a particular Sunday when his father rides down slave row as "his fateful appearance on the Street" (20). Why does he describe the incident in this way? How did it change Hiram's life?
13. When Thena learns that she and Hiram are going up to work in the big house, she warns Hiram that their lives, "'bout to get more brutal'" (21). This seems a strange thing to say. Explain Thena's reasoning.
14. What is ironic about the song that Hiram hears the field-hands singing as he walks up to the big house?
15. Of Lockless, Hiram says he feels, "This house ... belonged to me. It was mine

The Water Dancer by Ta-Nehisi Coates

by blood. I was correct, but not in the sense I thought" (22). Explain what he means.
16. Explain what "the Warrens" are (23). How does the architecture of Lockless function as a symbol of the separation of the races under slavery?

Summary:

Hiram's narrative jumps back to his childhood so that the reader gets the backstory to the accident. He recalls being "a strange child," able to talk before he could walk and possessing a photographic memory so he is able to "retrieve the exact images [of events] and translate them back into the exact words" (10). We learn that his experience in the water of Goose River is not Hiram's "first pilgrimage to the blue door" (11). The first occasion is when he is nine, the day after his mother is sold away. Realizing that he "*must get out*" (11), Hiram walks out before dawn one winter morning and feels a compulsion to go to the stables, "I was certain that something I could not name awaited me there, something crucial about my mother, some secret path, perhaps, that would send me to her" (12-13).

He is attracted to the water trough. Gazing into it, he feels a "blue mist … rising up out of the inky blackness" – just as he feels in Goose River (13). Then, inexplicably, he finds himself teleported back to the cabin he has just left. Here he becomes conscious that he can no longer remember his mother, "She'd gone from that warm quilt of memory to the cold library of fact" (14). He sleeps, and when he wakes Hiram realizes that he "was alone" as many slave children have discovered themselves to be (14). Instinctively, he makes his way to the cabin of Thena, a woman with a reputation for being mean, who takes him in. This is a strange choice for Hiram to make, but he instinctively empathizes with the sense of loss and pain that Thena is feeling. He admires her because she has "a rage that she, unlike the rest of us, refused to secret away, and I found that rage to be true and correct. She was … the most honest [slave in Lockless]" (15).

When he is eleven, a year and a half after Hiram moves in with her, Thena tells him about her husband, Big John, who was a field boss at Lockless, not because "'he was the meanest … [but] because he was the wisest – wiser than any of them whites, and their whole lives depended on him'" (17). John was particularly expert in the cultivation of tobacco, the staple crop at Lockless, but he died of a fever, and after his death the impoverishment of the soil led to one bad harvest after another. Thena watched helplessly as her five children were sold down Natchez. She tells Hiram that she knows the other enslaved people say she is "'broken,'" but she also knows that he sought her out to live with for a reason. She says she cannot take Rose's place as his mother, but she understands why he chose her.

Hiram has always known that his father is Howell Walker, the white master of Lockless; neither his mother (before she was sold) nor his father have made a secret of Hiram's paternity. Hiram feels how unfair it is that he does not have the same advantages as his white half-brother, Maynard, and looks to impress his father by displaying his phenomenal memory. One day, after dinner, Boss Harlan and his wife come to speak to Thena. After he leaves, Thena tells Hiram that he is going to work in the plantation house and that she is to go with him to tend to him. Thena warns him that his life is about to get more, not less, brutal than when he worked in the fields and tells him not to forget that the white people are not his true family. Together they go up to the big house where Hiram is first shown his windowless underground room and then taken to meet his father and half-brother in the library.

Analysis:

Hiram's experience the day after his mother is taken away helps to explain what happens to him in the waters of Goose River. Water seems to be the key to Conduction, for staring into the trough in the stable, Hiram feels the same blue door open. Looking into the water allows him to reconnect with "the Tasked who'd once lived down on the street but now were lost to me" (13). Time seems to disappear, and he is convinced that the water offers "a secret path that would deliver me from Lockless to reunite me with my mother" (13), but unable to control his superpower, it only transports him back to his cabin where he realizes the hard truth that he is alone and trapped in slavery. Hiram realizes that "amputation [from his past] must be immediate" (14), so he takes his possessions and rations to Thena's cabin. He chooses Thera because she is the only one on the street who will understand, "the suffering that was just then compounding in me" (15).

Thena tells Hiram that her husband's death, "'wasn't nothing natural ... It was murder'" (17). This illustrates the brutality of slavery in which people do hard manual labor, with little rest, and without proper medical care. Thena's meanness, scowling, and rages are the result of her helplessness to save either Big John or her five children. Unlike many of the other slaves, she does not live in denial by trying to forget these wrongs. In fact, she urges Hiram, "'though it hurt sometime, you cannot forget, Hi. You cannot forget'" (18). This only makes Hiram feel bad because he is unable to remember anything coherent about his mother; it is all just "smoke" (19). The unlikely bonding of Hiram and Thena shows how enslaved people form new relationships following forced family separation and how oral histories are passed from one generation to the next.

Thena's story of Big John again illustrates how the white masters come to rely not only on the muscle but also on the brains of their slaves. Howell depends totally on the income from tobacco production, but once John's expertise disappears, the plantation falls on hard times. Crop yields fall and therefore income falls, and Howell seems helpless. To the enslaved, the fields "'aren't just fields ... They the heart of the thing'" (17). This suggests an organic relationship between the field hands and the soil that the whites (who never come into contact with the soil) are incapable of feeling.

When Hiram sees his father, Howell Walker, riding through the Lockless plantation on his fine horse, Howell tips his hat at him. Although Hiram knows that Howell sold his mother, he cannot help but see the master as an aspirational figure, "in him, I saw an emblem of another life – one of splendor and regale" (19). Hiram is still too young to really appreciate the unbridgeable gulf between the

Quality and the Tasked, or to understand that, as the son of a slave, he inherits his mother's status, not that of his father. Hiram dreams of showing his father his "own quality" (20) as though by doing so he might find "my method, my token, my ticket out of the fields and off the Street" (21). The reader understands that he is deluding himself.

Howell openly acknowledges Hiram as his and shows him favor within the confines of what is acceptable to Virginia law and society. There is no reason to suppose that he does not have genuine affection for his illegitimate son, but he is also the master who sold Rose, leaving Hiram an orphan whom he keeps a slave. The master's small gestures of kindness (like smiling at him and throwing him a coin) create a naïve hope in Hiram that he will one day be able to escape slavery and live in luxury. Thena's reaction to the news that Hiram is wanted to work in the house is more realistic. She tells the boy that his life is. "'bout to get more brutal'" (21). Now historically the position of 'house negroes' was much better than that of field hands: their work was less physically demanding and they were generally dressed, fed and treated better. However, Thena tries to explain to Hiram that by going up to the house they will be losing their, "'own world down here – our own ways of being and talking and laughing'" (22). Paradoxically, they will be giving up what little freedom they have because the white people will always be watching them. In particular, she warns him not to mistake the master and his half-brother for his family because their blood ties mean nothing in the context of Quality and Tasked. Hiram is too young to understand. He writes, "We walked up from the tobacco fields, past the field hands" (22). Note the importance of the word "up" suggesting upward social mobility, and of "past" suggesting that Hiram feels he has overtaken the other Tasked, literally put them behind him. Ironically, the field hands are singing, "When you get to heaven, say you remember me" (22). Thena has already stressed the importance of memory to the enslaved; the danger is that Hiram will forget who he is and the African people from whom he comes.

When he first sees the big house up close, Hiram thinks, "It was all so magnificent. This house, I felt with a sudden shiver, belonged to me. It was mine by blood. I was correct, but not in the sense I thought" (22). The reader knows that Hiram's confident hope will never reach fruition. Lockless is his only in the sense that it has been built (literally) on the blood of his people. One of the Tasked can never become one of the Quality. Symbolically, Hiram is shown to his room which is part of a labyrinth of "adjoining tunnels … a warren, an underworld beneath the great house" (22). This is Hiram's place, not the library into which he is shown to meet his father and half-brother.

Chapter III

Notes:

"a bushel of apples" (25): i.e., a standard basket of apples holding about 125 medium apples.

"eight demijohns of cider" (26): A demijohn is a bulbous narrow-necked glass bottle typically enclosed in a protective wicker cover. In various sizes, they hold from three to ten gallons.

"catamounts" (34): i.e., a medium-sized or large wild cat, especially a cougar.

"*De Bow's Review*" (34): "*DeBow's Review* was a widely circulated magazine of 'agricultural, commercial, and industrial progress and resource' in the American South during the upper middle of the nineteenth century, from 1846 until 1884. Before the Civil War, the magazine 'recommended the best practices for wringing profits from slaves.'" (Wikipedia contributors. "De Bow's Review." *Wikipedia, The Free Encyclopedia*. Wikipedia, The Free Encyclopedia. 31 May. 2017. Web. 19 Dec. 2019.)

"entail" (34): i.e., the legally binding settlement of the inheritance of property over a number of generations so that it remains within a family – usually on the male side.

"put him on the block" (37): The slave block in Fredericksburg, Virginia, is a grayish-brown stone currently protruding from the sidewalk. It is about the size and shape of an overturned bucket. Slaves stood on it so that buyers could get a good look at them. Other towns had similar slave blocks.

"mahogany secretary" (38): A secretary desk, or escritoire, has a base of wide drawers topped by a desk with a hinged writing surface, over which is a bookcase usually with a pair of doors, often made of glass.

"Argand lamp" (38): i.e., a superior type of oil lamp, invented in 1780 by a Swiss, Aimé Argand.

"the Three Hills" (38): The only Three Hills I could find in Virginia is a historic home located near Warm Springs, Bath County, Virginia. But this was not built until 1913 and is too far west.

"Cupid … Aphrodite" (38): In Greek mythology Aphrodite (the Roman goddess Venus) is the mother of Eros (the Roman god Cupid).

"macabre rictus" (40): i.e., a frozen, fake smile.

"*The Christian Intelligencer*" (40): Previously entitled the *Magazine of the Reformed Dutch Church*, it was published in New York from 1830 to 1920.

"*The Register*" (40): The *Harrisonburg Rockingham Register Newspaper* was published in Harrisonburg, Virginia from 1825 to 1976.

"'put a passel on … bring home the whole acre'" (41): A passel (or parcel) is a quantity, part, or portion of the whole acre. He means that he will win a lot on his relatively small bet.

The Water Dancer by Ta-Nehisi Coates

Guiding Questions:

17. What indications of social change amongst the Virginia Quality are highlighted by Howell's social gathering (pages 24-27)?
18. What causes the Tasked in the waitstaff at the party to exhibit a "subtle tension" that the guests do not perceive (27)?
19. Why do you think that Howell wants to educate Hiram? Why is Hiram so anxious to agree to being taught by Mr. Fields – though, of course, he is very careful not to be "found too eager" (32)?
20. How does Hiram react when Howell tells him that his plan is to make him Maynard's manservant because, "'Maynard needs you at his side and it is your great honor to be there'" (37)?
21. What other strategy is Howell pursuing to ensure that, when he is dead, Maynard will be guided by a strong, sensible controlling hand?
22. Analyze the dream that Hiram had at the end of this chapter. What does it tell the reader of Hiram's unconscious thoughts?

Summary:

Hiram learns indirectly that his father wants him to make himself generally useful about the great house, and this he does in an effort to win Howell's favor. He rises before sunrise and helps wherever he is needed. There is always plenty to do because there are fewer slaves working in the house than in earlier, more prosperous, times – Hiram realizes that even house negroes may be sent to Natchez to be sold.

In the autumn of his thirteenth year, when Hiram has been in the house four months, Howell throws a party for the Virginia Quality. Ella, the head cook, complains about all the preparation she has to do. Hiram is one of the waitstaff. He is dazzled by the women's fashions and the men's distinction and grace, and he imagines himself "amongst them, settled into a chair or whispering in a lady's ear" (26).

Soon, however, the party degenerates into drunkenness. Alice Caulley slaps an enslaved man, demanding that he sing for them. Howell tells Alice that they "'have something better than any Negro song,'" and he turns to Hiram who instinctively knows what his father wants him to do (27). Hiram uses a deck of Maynard's reading cards and displays his ability to remember the rhymes written on each. Alice is amazed and delighted. Next, Hiram questions all of the guests about their lives and afterwards repeats their answers, with some added drama. The party ends in smiles and laughter.

The following day, Howell sends for Hiram, whom he introduces to Mr. Fields, Maynard's tutor. Howell asks him to spend some time with Mr. Fields, and Hiram politely agrees. Mr. Fields has been impressed by Hiram's memory tricks the previous evening and now gives him a variety of tests that he impressively passes. Mr. Fields shares the results with Howell, and the consequence is that Howell asks Hiram if he "'would like to work with Mr. Fields on some regular basis?'" (32).

Hiram politely agrees. Mr. Fields begins tutoring Hiram in literacy, math and oratory, and Hiram is thrilled by the new worlds this opens to him, and by the obvious fact that Mr. Fields prefers to teach him rather than Maynard, who is a poor student. Hiram allows himself to hope that he, not Maynard, will inherit Lockless and that this has been his father's plan all along.

Hiram studies with Fields for a year. Then, Howell tells him that he has long recognized his, "'particular talent'" (36) and that he wants him to be Maynard's personal servant because his heir, "'needs you by his side and it is your great honor to be there'" (37). Hiram spends the next seven years working as Maynard's manservant. When Hiram is nineteen, the day before the "fateful race-day," he is in Howell's study reflecting that he, not Maynard, is the man to restore the fortunes of Lockless (37). He knows that members of the Walker family also believe that Maynard will be the downfall of Lockless, but they know there is no other legitimate heir.

To further protect his legitimate son, Howell has arranged a marriage between Maynard and Corrine Quinn, "perhaps the wealthiest woman in all of Elm County." Rather like Hiram, Corrine is "superior to Maynard in every way," but as a woman alone she needs him because the gender norms of Virginia's patriarchal society mean that legally a man has to manage some aspects of her wealth and property (39). An overheard conversation between Howell and Maynard shows Hiram that his father talks to his brother in a way that he never talks to him and that they both unquestioningly support slavery and regard blacks as inferior.

Hiram is called into Howell's study where the master is talking to Maynard who is boasting about the winning bet he will make at the races and how it will make the Quality respect him. Howell is seventy and in decline. So many slaves have been sold that the house and plantation at Lockless seem deserted. When Maynard leaves, Howell repeatedly urges Hiram to take good care of him, and Hiram promises to do so. Howell seems to acknowledge the injustices that Hiram has suffered, but he shifts blame onto the hard times rather than take responsibility for his actions as a slave owner.

That night, Hiram has a nightmare in which the Tasked at Lockless are standing in the tobacco field. They are old and are chained to Maynard, who becomes a baby unaware of the people whom he holds chained. Everyone disappears until the only thing left is the night sky and the North Star.

Analysis:
Howell's social gathering illustrates much about the condition of the local Virginia Quality. Pete notes that falling yields have caused the 'old' slaveholding families to move west, to Natchez, Baton Rouge, or Tennessee, in search of fertile virgin land. Everyone attending this social knows that, "'This goodbye might be they last'" (25). We get the sense that the plantation system is in terminal decline.

The complaints of Ella, the head cook, that white people, "'don't think about nothing and nobody ... It's wrong'" show that Howell has no understanding of, or sympathy for, the hard work that his house negroes have to do to make his social gathering possible (25). Like all masters, he expects his black slaves to be continually cheerful, funny or entertaining. Hiram is happy to go along with this racial stereotype, writing of his pride that, "By then I had learned how to wash and groom myself until I shined" (26). He is impressed by the whites at his father's gathering, admiring the women's fashions and the men's distinction; he wants to be one of them. However, this sophistication is a thin veneer. Hiram notes that the pretense of gentility is very fragile, "While they played at aristocrats, we were their well-appointed and stoic attendants," but "Bored whites were barbarian whites." The Quality eat and drink too much and become quarrelsome. Alice Caulley's "broken mask of face-paint" is a fitting symbol for their superficial sophistication (27).

In this mood, the Quality turn to the Tasked to entertain them. Alice slaps a waiter and demands that he sing. Howell offers Hiram as an entertainment, "'better than any Negro song'" (27). The fact that Howell uses his son in this way is troubling, but Hiram willingly plays along. He interacts with the guests almost as if he is one of them. He boasts that he looks at Alice "longer than any tasking man should" and confidently requests the guests to line up (29). He appears not to notice that Alice repeatedly calls him "'boy'" (28-29) and that these people will never see him as their equal.

Hiram interprets his father's smile as a sign of his pride in Hiram's ability and is pleased. He records, but appears not to see the significance of, the fact that, though Howell treats him with studied politeness, he calls him by his name while he calls Maynard "'son'" (30). We notice Maynard's "relief" when Howell takes him away from "his work" so that the tutor can test Hiram (30). This is another example of the way in which the dependence that whites have on their black slaves results in the whites not preparing themselves to run their plantations and business affairs because they can get one of the Tasked to do it for them. Although he completely misunderstands his father's motives for having Fields teach him, in other ways Hiram shows how sensitive he is to his inferior position as one of the Tasked. He knows that "the Quality resented the pride of the Tasked, unless that pride could be fitted to their profit" (31). Thus, he feigns difficulty in performing Mr. Field's tests. When his father asks if he would like to work with the tutor, he knows he must not, "be found too eager ... [because] Lockless was still Virginia – the epitome even." However, this cannot obscure from the reader the error he is making in thinking that this offer, "was the avenue opening before me, light streaming through" (32). This description recalls the "blue door" that he experienced in Goose Rover. That *was* a true portal to freedom; the reader knows that his father's offer *is not* such portal.

It was most unusual for a master to educate a slave. Literacy among slaves was seen as dangerous because it encouraged private, even covert communication, freedom of thought, and knowledge of the outside world, and therefore rebellion.

Between 1740 and 1834, anti-literacy laws were passed in Alabama, Georgia, Louisiana, Mississippi, North and South Carolina, and Virginia. Howell's motives are hard for the reader to understand, and this makes Hiram's misunderstanding of them more natural. [The solution comes later: Fields is actually manipulating Howell to educate Hiram in ways that will make him a more useful agent of the Underground Railroad.]

Hiram now lives between two worlds. He knows himself to be more fitted to inherit Lockless than his half-brother and is convinced that his father also sees this. Howell shares with him the history of the Walkers and the building of Lockless and Hiram feels "as if granting [he is being granted] in these asides a teasing share of my inheritance" (33). Hiram fantasizes about inheriting the plantation and using his knowledge to reverse the decline in the family fortunes. At the same time, Hiram never forgets Thena's warning that the Walkers are *not* his family. He sees the brutality of Howell when Ella is abruptly sold. He observes for himself that Lockless, "would be lost without those who tasked within it." The big house is a machine designed to hide the fact that the Quality depend entirely upon the Tasked. Hiram realizes that though Maynard is "more profane" than the other whites, he is not "unoriginal." The privileged lives of the Quality are built on the "genius" of the Tasked, "Sloth was literal death for us, while for them it was the whole ambition of their lives" (35). Nevertheless, Hiram still deludes himself that someday his own "quality" (an interesting play on words by the author here) will be recognized, and he will be "deemed the true heir, *the rightful heir*, of Lockless" (36).

Hiram's hopes are dashed when his father tells him he is to become Maynard's manservant. Howell praises Hiram's intelligence, praises himself for not selling Hiram, and frames his proposal as an honor for Hiram. The reader suspects he is sincere: he is simple using a slave whom he thinks "'could be useful'" in the service of Lockless plantation without any thought about the slave's feelings (36). Looking back, Hiram writes, "It may seem strange now, but the insult of it did not immediately dawn on me. It accumulated slowly and inexorably over the years as I watched Maynard at work" (37). The fact that, despite his ineptitude, Maynard will inherit the running of Lockless highlights the irrationality of the racial division between the Quality and the Tasked.

On the day before the fateful horse race, Hiram reads a description of Oregon as, "'the seat of liberty, prosperity and wealth,'" and contrasts this with his own poverty and slavery – symbolized for him by "an engraving on the wall [depicting a] chained Cupid and a laughing Aphrodite" (38). Later, he overhears his father talking to Maynard about a local planter who took his slaves to Baltimore and freed them. Howell adds scornfully, "'Doubt they made it a week,'" though it was actually the planter who subsequently froze to death because he had no slaves to check on his horse in a snow storm (39). For the first time in the novel the reader learns that there are some white people, even in Virginia, who are sympathetic to abolition.

The Water Dancer by Ta-Nehisi Coates

Howell talks alone with Hiram. Sensing himself to be nearing death, he is more honest than ever before. For the first time, he admits that "'none of it [i.e., the system of slavery] is fair'" and calls Hiram "'son'" (43). However, Howell sees himself as the victim. He claims that, in what the system has allowed him to give Hiram, he has "'made it known how high you sit in my esteem'" (42-43), and bemoans the fact that he, "'must watch my people carried off, across the bridge and into God knows where'" (43). By this point, Hiram can see the hypocrisy of all this, just as he can see through the falsity of the smile Howell shows him. Howell sells human beings and denies Hiram the inheritance he is owed. That night Hiram has an epiphany. He reflects on Thena's warning: his privileged position as a house negro has kept him "from seeing the worst of our condition," and he feels for the first time "the crushing weight of seeing how the Quality truly lived, in all their luxury, and how much they really took from us" (43).

Hiram's dream symbolizes the injustice of being an enslaved person at Lockless. Maynard holds the chain, but "idling lost in his own thought," he is scarcely aware of doing so. Hiram identifies the North Star as, "the mark of my future days." The North Star was used by escaped slaves to find their way to the Free States. Notice that he sees it, "wreathed in brilliant but ghostly blue," a description that recalls the "blue door" he will experience next day in the waters of Goose River (44).

Chapter IV

Notes:

"Wellingtons" (49): i.e., knee-length leather boots popularized by Arthur Wellesley, 1st Duke of Wellington (1769-1852), the victor of the Battle of Waterloo (1815).

"Paducah" (49): The county seat of McCracken County, Kentucky.

"Ryland's Hounds" (54): A generic term for slave catchers who often used tracking dogs to sniff out runaways.

"the Underground" (55): This network of militant abolitionists operated from the late 18th century to the Civil War (April 12th, 1861 – April 9th, 1865).

Guiding Questions:

23. In what ways does Nathaniel Walker seek to hide the harsh reality of his sexual exploitation of Sophia?

24. Why exactly has Maynard been excluded from the society of the gentlemen of Quality? How does he hope to make them "at last acknowledge the merit of his blood" (54)? Why does he fail, and how does he react to his failure?

25. The celebratory atmosphere immediately after the races degenerates as the evening progresses into lawlessness and violence. As you read, make a list of the signs of this that Hiram records.

26. How did Georgie Parks become a free black man?

27. When Hiram asks for Georgie's help in escaping slavery, what two pieces of advice does Georgie offer?

28. How is Hiram's attitude to the Quality changed by his experience in town after the race meeting? What does he come to understand clearly for the first time about his fate if he stays at Lockless as Maynard's servant?

29. What triggers the apparition on the bridge?

Summary

The following morning, still shaken by his dream, Hiram gets water from the well and on the way back passes the room of Sophia who is knitting. This is her sole task since she is the mistress of her owner Nathaniel Walker, Howell's brother. Every weekend, Hiram drives Sophia, dressed like a lady of Quality, to the rear entrance of Nathaniel's house and later brings her back to Lockless. Nathaniel has Sophie watched at Lockless and makes it known that no Tasked men may show any interest in her. Being nineteen, Hiram feels he should be thinking about finding a wife, but he has seen too many loving couples separated to want to commit himself. Nevertheless, he is drawn to Sophia, and the feeling seems to be mutual. Sophia tells Hiram she has been imagining talking to him about race-day. Flirtatiously, she asks how she looks, and he replies, "'Not so bad, if I do say'" (48).

Hiram drives Maynard to Starfall for the races. All of the Quality are there, but they shun Maynard who, because of his awkwardness and rudeness, does not fit into their elegant world. Maynard attaches himself to Adelaide Jones, a woman (now married to a Northern lawyer) whom he once unsuccessfully courted. Adelaide is eventually detached from Maynard by a gentleman. Unable to mix with the Quality in the Jockey Club, from which he has been expelled, Maynard stands among the Low whites. He sees Corrine Quinn, who is in the ladies' section "elevated to a standing higher than his own," though she "spurned the ostentation of the parade" by dressing quite reservedly; Maynard feels "henpecked" by the sight of the woman he is to marry (51). Hiram joins the black people, some enslaved and some free. He nods to Corrine's servant Hawkins, who nods back but does not smile. Hiram finds him intimidating.

The races begin and Maynard's horse, Diamond, wins. He "exploded … screamed and embraced everyone around him" (53). The Quality, however, ignore him and that is why he later insists that Hiram drive him around the center of town, where the same snub is repeated. It is then that he decides to go the brothel. Alone for an hour, Hiram thinks about Sophia whom he loves and whom he thinks might return his love "in another world, a world beyond the Task" (54). Hiram further reflects that, given the economically depressed state of Virginia, it is no longer possible for a slave to earn enough to buy his/her freedom, as had happened in the past. The only other way to freedom, running, is "unthinkable … insane" because runaways are either caught by Ryland's Hounds or give up and come back (54-55). The only hope seems to be the largely mythical Underground that helps escaping slaves. He fantasizes that his acquaintance Georgie Parks is secretly an important member.

Suddenly, the festive air of Starfall turns into ugly riot. Hiram hears shots and sees an immaculately dressed white man firing his gun into the air; he witnesses a vicious knife fight; and sees two women fighting. This, Hiram reflects, is how Quality gentility always degenerates into riot, and he knows that the next stage will be to turn against the blacks. To avoid being caught up in trouble, he walks to Freetown, the separate "free colored" part of town. This area begins at Ryland's Jail, a prison for recaptured runaway slaves and those about to be sold. Thus, it is a constant reminder to the free blacks that they "existed in the shadow of an awesome power, which, at a whim, could clap them back in chains" (57).

At Georgie's house, Hiram is greeted as an old friend by Georgie's wife, Amber, who has a newborn son for whom Hiram has brought a carved wooden horse. Hiram asks Georgie how he felt the day he walked out of Lockless after buying his freedom, and Georgie says, "'Like a man. Which is not to say I wasn't one before, but I had never truly felt it'" (59). Georgie explains that freedom means having his own name, and getting up and going to bed when he wants to. Then he tells Hiram that all the men used to be in love with Rose because she was so beautiful and such a good dancer. Hiram envies Georgie his complete memory of the past.

Hiram tells Georgie that he feels he has to escape slavery: he is becoming a man; more and more of the Tasked are being sold down to Natchez; the soil in

Virginia has turned to sand; and the white people are increasingly lawless. He then tells Georgie he believes him to be a member of the Underground Railroad. Georgie tells Hiram that the only way out of slavery is to buy his freedom, as he did, but Hiram retorts that is no longer possible. Georgie then tells him, "'Then your life is your life. And may I say it is a good one. Your only charge is that dumb brother of yours. Go home, Hiram. Get yourself a wife. And make like you happy'" (61-62). Hiram leaves, but remains convinced that Georgie is testing him and determines to prove to his friend that he is worthy of helping.

As he walks back through town, Hiram sees that disorder has taken over: trash in the streets; a finely-dressed man unconscious, face-down in manure; the man's friends laughing at him; ruined clothing spread about; men playing dice; and others preparing for a cock fight. He finds Maynard, very drunk, standing outside the brothel with a fancy girl. Next to him is Hawkins, Corrine Quinn's servant. Maynard warns him not to tell Corrine about the fancy, and Hawkins leads him to believe that he will not. As he drives Maynard and the fancy back to Lockless, Hiram has another epiphany. He sees clearly that, when his brother is master of Lockless, Maynard will sell him down to Natchez. His vision of Rose water dancing comes as Hiram is feeling "a want, a desire for an escape from Maynard and the doom of his mastery" (64). He is still not sure how exactly Conduction works, but he knows that it is triggered by memory.

Analysis

Following his dream, Hiram's understanding of the cruel injustice of slavery deepens. As a young man, he would naturally be thinking of a wife, but relationships between the Tasked exist at the whim of the Quality. He has seen many "families formed in the shadow and quick, and then turned to dust with the white wave of a hand," and he knows that, should he have a wife and children, they too could be sold by Maynard whenever he wishes (46). This makes Hiram reluctant to form any attachment himself, but this decision is at odds with his feelings for Sophia. As a result, Hiram now understands that slavery not only robs him of his inheritance and the products of his labor, but even of his own romantic/sexual desires, "my own natural wants must forever be bottled up ... I must live in fear of those wants, so that more than I must live in fear of the Quality, I must necessarily live in fear of myself" (48).

Sophia is Nathaniel Walker's slave, and he uses the power of his ownership of her to coerce her to act as his "concubine." In return, Sophia gets an easier life since the only task she has to perform is knitting which she loves. Stripped of all the pretentions by which Nathaniel seeks to "transfigure robbery into charity," this is institutionalized rape (47). [The most famous example of such a relationship is that between Thomas Jefferson and his slave Sally Hemmings by whom he had several children.]

Hiram feels some sympathy for the way his brother is ostracized by the gentlemen: having been "unceremoniously ejected" from the jockey club because

54

of his uncouth behavior, he experiences "a world of painful longing" for his lost status (51). Hiram pities Maynard for his inability to live up to Virginia's image of a respectable gentleman.

Hiram reflects on the strange status of Low whites. The Quality tolerate them in public, but vilify them in private. These people have no connection with the Quality other than the color of their skin. They are desperately poor and condemned to the same brutal, dehumanizing labor as the Tasked, but they cling to the power of their whiteness, "They were a degraded and downtrodden nation enduring the boot of the Quality, solely for the right to put a boot of their own to the Tasked" (52).

As the economy of Virginia has declined due to falling tobacco harvests, so the condition of the Tasked has worsened. In the past, slaves might "save some small wage and then buy back their bodies," but now masters can make much more money by selling their slaves down South (54). As for running away, the Quality exploit the Low whites to catch escaped slaves, and even if they evade the hounds, the slaves lack knowledge of where to escape to. One distant hope is the Underground Railroad, but Hiram knows nothing about it except rumors. He, like other Tasked, fantasizes about "a secret society of colored men [who] had built their own separate world deep in the Virginia swamps" (55). Part of Hiram's fantasy is that his friend Georgie Parks, a highly respected free black man, is secretly a member of the Underground.

The sudden gun shots and the two fights that Hiram witnesses are further evidence that the veneer of civility is very thin among the Quality. It is a more severe form of what almost happened at Howell's social, "race-day would start in high pageantry, and then the drinking would start … and all the masks of fashion would fall away…" (56). The next stage of their meanness would be taken out on black people, and Hiram knows that free blacks are even more vulnerable that slaves who are under the protection of their master.

Georgie's life is poor, his cabin being scarcely better than that of a slave, but at least he has some dignity: he chooses his own name and decides what he wants to do. Yet the free blacks live literally in the shadow of Ryland's Prison, a constant reminder of the power of the whites. The prison is run by the Low, many of whom make good money, though they will never be accepted by the Quality. Hiram reflects again on the paradox that the Tasked hate the Low and vice versa, when they "should be in union and arrayed against the Quality" (57). Georgie tells Hiram that no one really gets out of slavery; although he is glad not to be one of the Tasked at Lockless, so long as the system endures, he will be a part of it because of his color.

Just before Hiram takes the great risk of sharing with Georgie his hopes of escaping, Amber comes in and says, "'Georgie filling you with lies? … Watch Georgie. He is slippery'" (60). Presumably this is meant to be light-hearted banter, but the author's use of juxtaposition is something a reader should consider. Georgie discourages Hiram's thoughts of escape and does not respond when Hiram suggests that he is a man who knows about the Underground Railway. Hiram is convinced that Georgie is just testing him, but the reader remembers his habit of wishful thinking.

Two new thoughts come to Hiram. The chaos and degradation he sees in town convinces him that the so-called "civilization" of the Quality is "a mask so thin that for the first time in my life, I wondered what I myself had ever aspired to… and not for the first time I saw that I had set my sights much too low … They were no better than us, and in so many ways worse" (62). Following the embarrassment of picking Maynard up outside the brothel, he realizes how his life will end if he stays at Lockless: "all paths led to Natchez" (63).

Conduction remains mysterious, particularly since Hiram, the mature narrator, admits that he does not "truly understand the entirety [of it]" (64). What is clear is that memory triggers an out-of-body experience in which the subject is physically removed from one space and teleported to another.

Chapter V

Notes:

"cotillions" (70): i.e., an 18th-century French dance which gave its name to a formal ball, especially one at which debutantes are presented.

"crinolines" (70): i.e., a petticoat of haircloth or other stiff material, worn under a full skirt to keep it belled out.

Guiding Questions:

30. Howell, the grieving father, believes several things about his dead son that are incompatible with the truth. What are they?
31. How does Sophia escape from the harsh realities of her life?
32. What is the significance for Hiram of finding his special coin out by the monument?

Summary:

Hiram is "in the water, and then falling into the light, guided by my dancing mother" (65). The next thing he knows, he is leaning on the memorial stone to Archibald Walker, the founder of Lockless and Hiram's great-grandfather, which is two miles from the river. Hiram spends three days in a fever before he regains consciousness and notices Sophia sitting near him, humming and knitting. At first Hiram is paralyzed, but slowly he regains movement in his body. He is aware that he is in Maynard's room, and when he wakes again, Howell is sitting there sobbing. Howell explains that they have not been able to recover Maynard's body. He grieves for Maynard because he always reminded him of his late wife. To Howell, his dead son was always compassionate; he tells Hiram that Maynard loved him and undoubtedly sacrificed himself to save Hiram. Hiram is staggered that his father can be so self-deluded but reflects that only in "the peculiar region of Virginia … where a man could profess his love for you one moment and sell you off the next" (70) could such "insanity" be believed (69).

Hiram returns to the Warrens. He hugs Thena, who remains undemonstrative. However, Sophia assures him that Thena constantly asked her for news of his condition and could not bring herself to see him because to do so would be too painful – a sure sign of her love. Hiram feels in his pocket for the coin his father gave him, but it is not there. Sophia tells Hiram that it was Hawkins who found him on the riverbank.

Unable to understand the contradiction between his memory of having been at the monument and Hawkins having found him on the river bank, Hiram walks out into the sunlight heading for the monument. However, he is inexplicably overcome by panic and returns to his room. That evening, he ventures out again. He encounters Sophia, and they walk together. He has noticed that she is often abstracted, and Sophia explains, "'Sometimes a thought carry me away and I forget where I am. Come in handy sometimes…'" (74). Hiram tells her of the "'big dumb dreams'" he had when he first came up to the house, and she tells him about her life in Carolina before she was brought to Virginia. She had a husband there, Mercury, and they loved to dance. Although he admits that he did not inherit his mother's talent for dance, Sophia says his quiet ways remind her of Mercury. Sophia admits she does not know why she is telling Hiram so much about herself, but he reflects that people are always telling him their stories.

The next morning, Hiram walks to the monument where he finds his coin – proof that he was physically there on the night of the accident.

Analysis:

Hiram's immersion in water is a symbolic baptism and his waking from three days of unconsciousness a symbolic resurrection (think of Jesus). We expect to find him a new man, and indeed Hiram's understanding of the perverse effects of slavery does seem to be more mature as he reflects that his father's erroneous beliefs about his son's character are simply an extension of the lies that the Quality tell themselves about their relationship with the Tasked. The reader notes that Howell does call Hiram his son, but that is only when they are alone together.

For the Tasked, present reality is often unbearable. Sophia has no superpower to transport her to another place, but she uses the power of her mind to get lost inside a thought so that her mind is dissociated from her body. The reader imagines her using this to block out the reality of being raped by the man who owns her.

Evidently Sophia is attracted to Hiram. She teases him saying that seeing him sick, "'was hard even on me, and I don't like you, much less love you'" (71). Hiram gets the message and says his heart tumbles in his chest. Interestingly, Sophia has no hesitation telling Hiram about her earlier marriage to Mercury and how much fun they had dancing. From what she says, Mercury may well still be alive, but he is irretrievably lost to her. Hiram respects her memories for he knows how important the past is to the Tasked.

The coin that Howell gave him was once his "token into the Realm"; that is, he had thought that it would give him access to the world of the Quality. Now, however, he understands that it is a token, "but not [into] the Realm I'd long thought" (77). The coin is Hiram's proof that Conduction is real and that it has the ability to take him out of slavery.

Chapter VI

Notes:
"Adams secretary" (80): Robert Adam (1728–1792) was an architect and furniture designer who introduced a neoclassical style of interior design and architecture.
"highboy" (80): i.e., a high chest of drawers.

Guiding Questions:
33. In what ways is the work that Hiram does on the mahogany highboy different from the tasks he normally performs at Lockless?
34. Corrine's behavior is hard to understand. For example, the attitudes that she expresses toward Maynard are completely inconsistent. What is she up to?
35. Explain the similarities between the story of Santi Bess and the forty-eight slaves and the two experiences that Hiram has had.
36. Falling in love with Sophia, and knowing that she returns his love, appears to foreshadow problems and conflicts for Hiram. What are they?

Summary:
The exertion, both physical and mental, takes a toll on Hiram, and he begins to feel faint. Thena finds him, admonishes him for overdoing it, and takes him back to the Warrens to rest. The next day, Roscoe similarly urges Hiram to rest because they will work him hard again soon enough. However, Hiram craves the escape from his disturbed thoughts that working will be bring him, so he goes to the shed where Howell keeps furniture waiting to be restored. He selects a mahogany highboy and begins sanding it. Even when Thena sees him and orders him back to bed, he continues because, "It was the most peace I'd had in days, as a kind of mindlessness fell over me" (81).

The next morning, Hiram finishes his project. Hawkins, Corrine Quinn's manservant, approaches and says that his mistress would like to speak with him. Hiram has noticed that since Maynard's death, Corrine has regularly visited Howell to lead him in prayer, and he finds Corrine with Howell. They are "speaking of Maynard, sharing in their longing for him, or at least some beautified version of him, for this Maynard – held by them as a sinner on the verge of repentance – was not one I recognized" (82). Howell leaves him with Corrine and her servants, Hawkins and Amy. Hiram belatedly thanks Hawkins for saving his life, but Hawkins modestly replies that Hiram got himself out of the river and onto the grass where he found him.

Corrine states that, by her marriage to Maynard, they would all have been family, and that she wants this despite Maynard's death. She says she has heard Howell speak of Hiram's "genius that must be hidden from [the Quality]" lest it cause envy (83). Corrine's claim to *know* him disturbs Hiram, for the Quality do not speak like this to the Tasked; slavery only works when the masters make no effort to know as people the slaves they command. He wonders whether she somehow knows about his Conduction. Deeply uneasy, Hiram evasively says something complimentary about Maynard, but Corrine stops him saying, "'Put no flattery upon my ears, boy'" (83).

Corrine admits all of Maynard's faults but claims to have loved him despite them and to be "'broken'" by his death. Hiram tends to believe that her sorrow is genuine, except that then she paints a romanticized picture of Maynard's relationship with Hiram, "'You were his right arm, and without his guidance and protection, I wonder what you now make of yourself'" (85). She uses emotional blackmail to pressurize Hiram into giving a heroic account of Maynard's death, and Hiram obliges with lies because he hopes that they will comfort her.

Corrine then asks what Hiram will do now, and he replies realistically, "'I go where I am called, ma'am'" (86). Corrine suggests he might be called to work for her. Only later does Hiram conclude that the "grief and weeping might be true, but more certain was her dark intent – to pry me from Lockless and claim my services, my body, as her own" (87). Hiram feels that he has been manipulated and that his future is out of his hands: as property, Howell might pass ownership to Corinne, and she could take him away not only from Lockless, the only home he has ever known, but also from Elm County (and from Sophia, though he does not think so far ahead).

Maynard's body is not found, so it is decided to hold a Walker family gathering at Christmas in his memory. The Tasked at Lockless work hard restoring the big house and the slave quarters to receive all of the guests. For Hiram, this is a happy time because the work "forced all the difficult and thorny questions from my mind," and because the reunion means he gets to see black people whom he knew as a child (88). On Christmas Day, half of the Tasked prepare the feast for the Quality and half prepare the feast for the Street. Afterward, sitting around a fire, the slaves talk about the way the Walkers now speak kindly of Maynard who in his life they despised. Thena cuts in with the truth, "'It's his bequest they after. Land, niggers. Land and us! This whole thing is a game and the winner gets to take hold of this place, get to take hold of us'" (90-91). She speaks out of the particular bitterness of her own suffering and walks away.

The talk around the fire turns to the familiar story, whether history or myth, of Hiram's grandmother, Santi Bess, who led forty-eight enslaved people into the River Goose who all "reemerged on the other side of the sea" in Africa. Georgie Parks says that he *knows* the story to be untrue. Privately, Hiram agrees it is "preposterous," but the others challenge how Georgie can be so sure. Georgie seems uncomfortable, and they get no answer (92).

Spontaneously, people start playing music and dancing. Sophia gets up to water dance. Seeing Hiram, she dances over and gives him the jar to drink. He is shocked to find it is ale, but drinks it all and returns it to her. Hiram is aware that this action is the beginning of a courting ritual. The two walk to a gazebo near the ice house. Hiram knows he loves Sophia, "All I was thinking about was the light dancing in me, dancing to some music I hoped only she would hear" (95).

The Water Dancer by Ta-Nehisi Coates

Analysis:

The novel has repeatedly challenged the Southern stereotype of the slave as by nature ignorant, lazy and dishonest – a stereotype that was used to justify coercion to make slaves work. Instead, Hiram has described black field hands who have an intimate relationship with the soil; black builders who created the beautiful plantation homes; and black cooks who produced all of those Southern delicacies. As Georgie Parks has said, the difference is not the labor that free blacks do but the fact that they *choose* what to do and when to do it. Hiram has always been a hard worker, and at a time when he is psychologically troubled, he instinctively turns to manual work as therapy. In choosing to restore an antique, he selects a task in which he is able to use his skills, intelligence, creativity, and above all his own judgment. Although he is ultimately working for Howell's benefit, this is as close as a slave can get to working for his own satisfaction.

Corrine is a mystery – to the reader as well as to the young Hiram. The black veil that she wears effectively prevents both Howell and Hiram from looking into her eyes; it is a mask. Her recent visits to Lockless seem to be aimed at manipulating Howell, and she expertly manipulates Hiram. At times, she is surprisingly honest, as when she lists Maynard's faults, but then to both Howell and Hiram she reverts to a romanticized version of Maynard. Then again, she employs a common euphemism when she tells Hiram that, had she married Maynard, she and he would have been 'family'. The reader knows that Maynard never regarded Hiram as his brother. We remember Thena's warning before she and Hiram went to the big house, "'They ain't your family, boy. I am more your mother standing right here now than that white man on that horse is your father'" (22). This euphemism is just another of the dishonest ways in which the Quality obscure the realities of ownership under a civilized veneer.

In reacting to Corrine's familiarity, Hiram explains that "the Quality … did not inquire on the inner workings of their 'people'" (83). In fact, the masters do not see slaves as being 'people' in the same sense as they themselves obviously are. Slavery is a dehumanizing institution. Hiram concludes, "there is but one way to ensure that a man takes … care in a process that rewards him nothing, and that way is torture, murder, and maiming, is child-theft, is terror" (84). This is powerful writing, and it has the added virtue of being true, but the reader must begin to ask if the author is not over-using his protagonist as his propagandist.

What is Corrine up to? Obviously, the author leaves the reader to speculate. Corrine wants Hiram, but why? Is it possible that, through Hawkins, she knows that Hiram's genius includes the ability to move through space-time? Is she simply playing the grieving 'widow' for the power it gives her over Howell (and so over Hiram), or is her grief genuine? This chapter certainly foreshadows a move away from Lockless for Hiram, but to where, and how will a move impact his budding relationship with Sophia? Plenty of 'hooks' here to motivate the reader to read on!

The preparations for the Christmas holidays show the capacity of the enslaved to create happiness even in the most oppressive of circumstances. The myth of

Santi Bess shows the importance of oral history to the Tasked, most of whom cannot read or write. It also shows the importance of hope: they need to believe that escape is possible. Although Hiram, like Georgie, finds the story contrary to reason, the reader sees a connection with his own two experiences of Conduction that he appears not to make.

Sophia's water dance connects her with Rose and Emma. When he sees her turning away men who approach her, Hiram fails to understand that the only man she wants is him. As they sit together gazing up at the stars, he wonders how he could ever have endured driving her to her assignations with Nathaniel Walker and worries that Corrine's plans could soon take him away from Lockless. The future is full of "all the terror that came with" loving her, but for the moment Hiram is just lost in that love (95).

Chapter VII

Notes:

"Mordred ... the Dragon, in Camelot's clothes" (100): Mordred, sometimes called the Dragon Prince, was one of the Knights of the Round Table, but he betrayed King Arthur. He fought Arthur at the Battle of Camlann, where he was killed and Arthur fatally wounded.

Guiding Questions:

37. What are the main factors motivating Sophia to suggest escaping to Hiram?
38. Describe how Georgie responds when Hiram comes to him to ask for his help in escaping with Sophia.
39. What is foreshadowed by the narrator's comment that Georgie, "must have been figuring on the consequences of such an action, and ... he saw but one path forward" (103).

Summary:

In the new year, having seen Hiram's work on the highboy, Howell gives him the task of restoring old furniture. Reading the documents of sale for each piece gives Hiram insight into his ancestry on his father's side. Yet he knows that he is likely to be taken away from Lockless and that he will be unable to save the plantation, so his thoughts turn to freedom and again to Georgie Parks.

When Hiram is driving Sophia to Nathaniel's house, she tells him that she was raised with Nathaniel's wife, Helen, whose maid she became. The two grew up together, were best friends, and loved each other. Sophia implies that Nathaniel seduced her before Helen died in childbirth, and she still feels overcome with guilt. She tells Hiram that Nathaniel regards her as just a piece of "'jewelry'"; he will discard her when she is "'used up'" and turn to a younger black woman (99). She dreads getting pregnant and bringing a child, perhaps a daughter, into this world. This leads her to suggest that the two escape together. She explains that she is telling this to Hiram because, having survived drowning, she does not see how he can continue to live as a slave, and because his knowledge of the wider world must have made him want to see that world. They arrive at Nathaniel's house, and as Sophia goes inside, for the first time, she looks back at him. He remembers, "I knew then, looking at her, that we must run" (101).

Hiram still sees Georgie as the key to escape. He explains Georgie's reluctance as a result of a fatherly concern for him, particularly since he has seen so many runaways caught and sent to Natchez. The next day, Hiram visits Georgie, who receives him without a smile because he knows why Hiram is there. They walk. Georgie tells Hiram how much he likes and admires him, but adds that he cannot understand why Hiram, "'would come to my door looking for trouble.'" He repeats his advice to Hiram, "'Go home. And get a wife. And get happy.'" Hiram insists that he intends to escape and will take Sophia with him. This shocks Georgie even more. Georgie warns him that taking, "'Nathaniel Walker's girl ... is a high offense against any white man's honor'" (102). Hiram angrily rejects the idea that Sophia belongs to Nathaniel, but Georgie states the reality that every enslaved person Hiram knows belongs to white people, and that even he, Georgie, is not truly free. Nevertheless, Hiram insists that he is getting out. Reluctantly, Georgie tells him to come to the same spot in one week with Sophia.

Leaving Georgie, Hiram cannot avoid Amy and Hawkins. Hawkins asks why he is in town and if it is to see Georgie. Hiram is suspicious: Hawkins may be one of those blacks whose task is to spy on others and report suspicious activity to the masters. Next, Hiram notices Mr. Fields walking toward Amy, but seeing Hiram, Fields seems to hesitate and consider a change of direction, and Hawkins also appears uneasy. However, Fields merely tips his hat to Hiram, and Hawkins becomes his polite self again. Nevertheless, it is a troubling encounter: Hiram wonders what Corrine, Amy, Hawkins, and Mr. Fields are up to.

The next day, going to Nathaniel's estate to collect Sophia, Hiram encounters Ryland's Hounds, Low whites looking for runaways. They do not detail him because he has documents from Howell, but they make Hiram nervous because he already thinks of himself as a fugitive. On the way back to Lockless, Sophia tells him she has to escape, and he replies, "'Then let's get out'" (107).

Analysis:

Hiram cannot help being interested in the story of his (white) ancestry. He has an affection for Lockless as something that his people built – both the white masters and the black slaves. But he also knows that the family line will end with him, a slave sold away. Similarly, Sophia grew up loving Helen (and being loved by her), though their relationship changed when they were adults and became mistress and maid. Hiram considers, "It is a cruel thing to do to children, to raise them as though they are siblings, and then to set them against each other so that one shall be queen and the other shall be a footstool" (98). The same might, of course, be said of his own position in relation to Maynard.

Hiram calls slavery "a kind of fraud, which paints its executioners as guardians at the gate, staving off African savagery, when it is they themselves who are savages" (100). Nathaniel's weekly rape of Sophia is an example that must rankle the more because he drives her to and from it.

Georgie's statement that Sophia belongs to Nathaniel sparks real anger in Hiram. This is because it makes him realize, for the first time, that he really does love Sophia. Looking back, he comments, "when I did feel that I loved her, it was not with reason and ritual, nor the way that makes families and homes, but the way that wrecks them, I was undone" (103). Georgie's attitude is hard to understand. He seems entirely defeatist about slavery. This does not fit with Hiram's conviction that Georgie is involved with the Underground, but what if Hiram (and everyone else who believes this) is wrong about Georgie? How might a free black man respond to learning about two slaves planning to escape? There is a hint of an answer when Hiram, the mature narrator, comments that Georgie, "must have been figuring on the consequences of such an action, and … he saw but one path forward" (103). These are fine examples of the author's use of foreshadowing.

Hiram suspects Hawkins of having lied about where he found him on the night Hiram almost drowned in the Goose. As a result, he mistrusts the man, as he mistrusts Corrine. There is just something that does not fit, in Hiram's experience about "the familiarity between two tasking folks [Hawkins and Amy] and a learned man of the North [Mr. Fields]. I should have seen the connections with Georgie Parks" (106). In this further piece of foreshadowing, the mature narrator hints at the mistake Hiram is making.

Chapter VIII

Notes:

"drunkard's chair" (109): A wide upholstered armchair popular in 18th century England that got its name because it had large, stable, feet to stop the sitter overbalancing.

"Hepplewhite table" (109): George Hepplewhite (c.1727-1786) was an English cabinetmaker who produced a distinctive style of light, elegant furniture fashionable between about 1775 and 1800.

"Queen Anne clock" (109): An elegant longcase clock from the early eighteenth century. Anne was Queen of England, Scotland, Wales and Ireland between March 1702 and May 1707.

"Ramsay and Morton" (117): The Reverend James Ramsay (1733-1789) was a ship's surgeon, Anglican priest, and leading abolitionist. He was the author of *An Essay on the Treatment and Conversion of African Slaves in the British Sugar Colonies* (1784) and *An Inquiry Into the Effects of Putting a Stop to the African Slave Trade: And of Granting Liberty to the Slaves in the British Sugar Colonies* (1784). Samuel George Morton (1799-1851) was an American physician and natural scientist, whose work argued that man was divided into distinct races. He was the author of *Crania Americana; or, A Comparative View of the Skulls of Various Aboriginal Nations of North and South America: To which is Prefixed An Essay on the Varieties of the Human Species* (1839).

Guiding Questions:

40. Sophia tells Hiram, "'Just get me out of here and I'll get the rest figured myself'" (111). Explain what she means by this.

41. Why does Hiram react so angrily when Thena tries to tell him that his association with Sophia cannot end well?

42. What clues are/have been given to explain Georgie's motivation in betraying Hiram and Sophia?

Summary:

Hiram, the mature narrator, recaps the reasons he needed to run and the part his feelings for Sophia played in his decision. From this perspective, of course, he can see the errors that he made in judging people and situations. Specifically, he admits that it would all "have made more [sense] had I considered that Sophia was a woman of her own mind, with her own intentions, calculations, and considerations of her own" (108-109).

Sophia comes to see Hiram in the shed where he is working and asks if they can discuss the plan for their escape. They meet an hour later in the privacy of the woods. While he waits, Hiram thinks only of Sophia and freedom. Sophia wants details, but Hiram admits that he is simply trusting Georgie and the Underground to take them to another world in the swamps where black people can live free. Sophia says, "'Just get me out of here and I'll get the rest figured myself'" (111).

Hiram is shocked by the word *myself*, so Sophia explains that she will not be controlled by Hiram like she has been by Nathaniel. She wants freedom, not another form of servitude. Hiram understands that Sophia fears being tied to a man who will effectively make a slave of her, so he promises that if they form a relationship it will be by her free choice. He shares with her what freedom means to him.

Returning alone to the Warrens, Hiram encounters Thena. Now that he has decided to run, he looks differently at Thena and the other Tasked: he is angry that they know how Lockless will end and what their own fate will be, but they do nothing about it. Thena challenges him about running around with "'Nathaniel Walker's girl'" implying that he is still fevered (114). For the first time, Hiram gives Thena a cutting look and speaks back to her, asking what right she has to speak to him like that. Thena claims the right of a mother who cared for him as a child and warns that he will come to regret both his actions and the way he has talked to her. At the time, however, Hiram is sure he will leave everything behind "for the freedom of the Underground, and [he] made no exception for Thena" (115).

On the day of the planned escape, Hiram goes to the well conscious that he is seeing people for the last time. He watches Thena laboriously washing laundry, and feels ashamed of having scorned and disrespected her, but he suppresses these thoughts with anger against her and avoids a meeting. Later, Howell, who has told him to start working in the kitchen next day, tells Hiram he has, "'One last day of freedom'" (116).

That evening, Hiram walks through the woods with Sophia to meet Georgie. Near the place, they hear footsteps and conversation. Hiram is reassured when he hears Georgie's voice, but when he emerges Georgie's "face was pained and was sad and I did not know why" (118). Five white men appear, one holding a rope. Sophia moans, "'No, no, no,'" and the white men tell Georgie he has "'done good'" (119).

Analysis:

We have already learned that the Virginia Constitution and the unwritten rules of the Quality meant that Corrine needed to have a husband in order to run her affairs effectively because there were certain things that a woman just could not do. Further, we have learned that Nathaniel was unfaithful to his wife, Helen, with her maid, Sophia. Now Sophia is used to alert the reader to the double slavery of black women: bound by a chain to the master and subservient by patriarchy to her man. For Sophia it makes no sense to secure freedom from only one of these two forms of bondage.

The mature narrator has made it clear that Hiram has made mistake after mistake and is heading for a fall. Hiram's self-confidence is thus less than admirable. He feels himself superior to all of the older slaves because he has not given up on freedom, but he is only nineteen and they have a wisdom from experience that he lacks. His arrogance to Thena is unpardonable and the mature narrator notes, "I was a child, I know that now, a boy overrun with emotion, undone by a great and momentous loss" (114). What he means by this is that running away will involve leaving a second mother and he has not the courage to tell her, so he reacts with anger.

There is an unconscious irony in Howell's use of the phrase, "'One last day of freedom,'" given that Hiram plans for this day to be his last in servitude (116). Another irony lies in Howell's use of the word 'freedom' to describe Hiram's period of recuperation: Hiram has had some control of how he spent his time, but he has still been a slave working for his master-father's benefit.

Georgie's reason for betraying Hiram and Sophia are not explained, but it is clear that he takes no pleasure in what he does or in the approval of the Low. As a free black, Georgie's position is still precarious. He cannot afford to become connected with any action intended to subvert the authority of the Quality over the Tasked.

Chapter IX

Guiding Question:

43. What is unusual about the way that the Low slave catchers treat their two captives?

Summary:

Ryland's Hounds tie Hiram and Sophia up and march them to Ryland's Jail at gunpoint. Hiram has feared that they might rape Sophia and beat him because that is what normally happens, "It was the necessary right of the Low, who held no property in man, to hold momentary property in those who ran, and vent all their awful passions upon them" (120). Surprisingly, this does not happen.

In jail, Hiram feels the metaphorical chains in which he has always lived replaced by real chains. He desperately tries to apologizes to Sophia, but she says nothing, and he wishes he had a knife to cut his throat. Sophia drags herself closer to Hiram, and he believes she wants to injure him, but she looks at him with tenderness and then gazes toward Freetown. Hiram knows that she too dreams of killing herself. Instead, she leans against him, and the warmth of her body frees him from his fears.

Analysis:

The relatively restrained behavior of Ryland's Hounds is unexplained and intriguing.

The tender moment that Hiram and Sophia share in their time of greatest trial is a reminder that slaves are human beings.

PART TWO

Chapter X

Notes:

"the fancy trade" (125): i.e., sold into prostitution.

"phrenology" (126): Phrenology was a pseudoscience, based on the theories of Viennese physician Franz Joseph Gall (1758-1828), which held that bumps on the skull were predictive of mental traits and character.

"river James" (131): The James River in Virginia rises in the Appalachian Mountains and flows into Chesapeake Bay. On its banks was founded Jamestown, the first English settlement to survive.

"varmint trap" (132): i.e., a trap for a troublesome wild animal.

"a coffle of coloreds" (134): i.e., a line of slaves, fastened and driven along together.

"Marvell's Book of Wonders" (137): From the context, this appears to be an encyclopedia, but (surprisingly) I was unable to identify the particular reference. Or is Coates making a joke about Marvel Comics?

Guiding Question:

44. In what ways does Hiram's incarceration allow the author to present aspects of slavery that he has not previously been able to dramatize?

Summary:

Next day, Sophia disappears. Hiram hates Georgie and dreams of revenge, though the mature narrator notes that later he would understand, "the way the Quality had narrowed his choices until he lived on a thin chancy reed called Freetown" (125). Hiram is forced to exercise and wash every day, then is taken out to be examined by Natchez slave traders, Low men of uncouth habits who, despite their wealth, are shunned by the Quality, whose God, "held that those who would offer a man for sale were somehow more honorable than those who affected that sale" (126). During their invasive probing of his body (which he understands to be a form of rape), Hiram escapes into his memories.

Hiram shares a cell with a boy of about twelve and an old man. The latter is much more cruelly treated by the white guards. The narrator explains, "The math of profit shielded me and the boy. But this old man, his days of use over, with only pennies to be wrung for him, was meat for the dogs" (127). Hiram is ashamed that he can do nothing to help the man. The boy's mother, a free black who has somehow lost custody of her own child, comes to visit and they hold hands through the bars. Hiram finds the scene reminiscent of his parting with his own mother.

One night, the old man tells Hiram his story. He recalls the old times, before the soil gave out, when the Tasked generally had the stability of remaining with their families. Hiram has heard stories of a time when Virginia was prosperous and the lives of slaves were more bearable, but feels that they make slavery seem acceptable. The man, who tells Hiram that his name does not matter, was once happily married and had a son, an upright, intelligent, skilled man whom everyone respected and who hoped thereby to be granted his freedom – very like Hiram's own dreams, and just as unrealistic. Before the man's wife died of fever, she made him promise to keep their son safe. The son got married to an "'honorable'" girl who "'was like the spirit of his mother returned,'" and they had three children, two of whom died in infancy (130-131). When tobacco yields began to fall, slaves were sold Natchez-way to make up the loss, and the plantation headman regretfully informed the man that his son, wife and child were to be sold. However, the slave traders had no use for the woman, and they did not take her. Both she and the old man sank into despair – he because he had failed to keep his promise to his dying wife. In their grief, the father and his son's wife eventually lived together as man and wife. He tells Hiram that he, "'will not disavow it … will not denounce her'" (133). Years later, the old man's son was, quite by chance, brought back to the area by his current master. Life being intolerable, in an act of defiance, the old man set fire to the plantation cookhouse, knowing what the consequences would be. He cries, fearful of how his first wife will turn away from him in the afterlife. Hiram can only put the man to bed.

The boy is taken away – his mother walking alongside the wagon for as long as she can. Later, she returns to Ryland's Jail, "crying out, inconsolable, summoning the wrath of God" (135). The white guards beat her and drag her off as Hiram watches, helpless to intervene. The old man is taken out one night by the guards and never returns. Hiram spends three weeks in the jail, starved and thirsty, forced to labor in the hardest, most degrading tasks. This makes no sense to him since he is, "young and strong as should have fetched a price within days" (136). Finally, Hiram is dragged out in chains, blindfolded, and gagged to be inspected by his purchaser. After a long carriage ride, he is unbound and pushed into a dark pit for the night. There, he remembers tales of white men who buy blacks just to torture and kill them.

Analysis:

From occupying what many would call a privileged place at Lockless because of his mixed race, Hiram has descended to "the coffin of slavery," that of a chained runaway being sold South (127). Just as Sophia's body has been regularly penetrated by Nathaniel, so now the vile slave traders poke into every orifice to judge the value of his body, and just as Sophia did, he disappears into his own thoughts to avoid the humiliating reality.

In the prison cell, Hiram is confronted by two examples of family separation. Like himself, the boy is going to be separated from his mother at an early age. The old man's son, also like Hiram in that he harbored unrealistic hopes that he might be able to obtain his freedom as a result of his obvious merits, was sold down Natchez. The young husband was born in the days of Virginia's prosperity when family separation was uncommon. Understandably, his father speaks almost with nostalgia of those better times, but Hiram takes an absolutist position feeling that, "There was no peace in slavery, for every day under the rule of another is a day of war" (130). Of course, he is young and never experienced those days himself.

The old man's coupling with his daughter-in-law, a betrayal of both his late wife and his son, is easy to condemn – indeed, it is the kind of story whites use to 'prove' that blacks have no morals. However, the man's defense is important. He says he has, "'sinned in a world of terrible sinners … [in a world that] is constructed to divide father from son, son from wife, and we must bite back with whatever a blade we have to hand'" (133). The man's sin, if it *was* a sin, is as nothing compared to brutal, dehumanizing, profoundly immoral institution of slavery itself, and he has paid a terrible and disproportionate price both in his religious conscience and in the daily beatings and humiliation to which he is subjected by the white guards.

The distraught mother who returns to the Jail, is not one of those blacks who endure their suffering "with dignity and respect," and this seems right to Hiram. How absurd it is to "cling to morality when surrounded by people who had none" (135) – more than that, to do so is almost like complicity in the crime. Hiram's experiences in this part of the novel expand his understanding of slavery since they take him from the relatively privileged position he had at Lockless to the lowest depths of degradation.

Chapter XI

Guiding Questions:
45. Hiram is finally taken out of the pit and put onto a wagon. Speculate on what you think the white men have in store for him.
46. Why do you think that the man who owns Hiram speaks in the way that he does to the black 'criminals' just before the first hunt?
47. At the end of the chapter the air opens up. Through a hole in time and space, Hiram escapes his hunters. What do you now understand about the preconditions for such an event to occur?

Summary:
In the pit, cut off from all light, Hiram loses track of time, and cannot distinguish between dreams and memories. He recalls that in his first year as Maynard's man, his half-brother "had the perverse notion to gather all the Tasked up" and make them run races in the hot August sun for his amusement (138). Hiram, who "had not yet understood my place among things," was shocked when Maynard ordered him to race too and share their "humiliation" (139). Hiram remembers running fast, then tripping and limping for three weeks.

Without food or water, an indeterminate time passes until the entrance to the pit opens and a ladder is dropped down. Hiram is commanded to climb out; it is dusk. The "ordinary" man who bought him has bizarrely placed two chairs and table and motions Hiram to sit, but he refuses. The man throws Hiram packages of bread, and Hiram drinks from a jar of water. He reflects, "I had never truly experienced hunger until my time down in that pit" (140).

A wagon approaches and the ordinary man orders Hiram inside where he joins other black men. Like Hiram, they are not chained, but chains are not necessary to hold these men, for they have been "broken." They drive for an hour, and the man orders them out. He is only one man, but Hiram reasons that "white men in Virginia are never really alone" (141). Three other carriages pull up, and a number of Low men get out. The ordinary man begins listing the supposed crimes of each of the black men, though some deny their guilt. He says they, "'are now in the care of these Virginia gentlemen,'" who will give them a certain time to run. If the black men can evade their pursuers all night, they will be freed, but if caught, their "'whole life is at their [hunters'] mercy'" (143).

The ordinary man drives off leaving the black men "too stunned to move" (143). A Low white hits one of them over the head with a cudgel, and he collapses in agony. The others, including Hiram, run – each man for himself. Hiram runs without knowing where to: North is, "but a word," and the Underground, "a myth spread by that villain Georgie Parks" (144). Still he runs, but his physical weakness lets him down; he falls in the mud and is recaptured and brutally beaten. The ordinary man repossesses him and takes him back to the pit. The whole hunt is repeated regularly with the same result. It is like, "the hell of which my father spoke," and his only escape is into memories (147).

Night by night, Hiram gets mentally stronger: running itself is "a kind of defiance" (146). He grows more skilled at evading the hunters and sometimes almost makes it to dawn. Almost! Hiram realizes that what he needs is the ability to "fly" as he had twice before, once from the stables to the loft of his cabin and once from the river to the memorial. He begins to analyze those incidents and comes to the conclusion that they were both connected to the memory of his mother, Rose. He concludes that they, "must have some relation to my mother ... to the block in my memory, and to unlock one was, perhaps, to unlock the other" (147). Hiram tries to remember everything he can about Rose.

The next time he runs, Hiram can hear the hunters closing in when he comes to a pond. Trying to get around it he trips, reinjures his ankle, and falls in. In agony, and knowing he is about to be taken, Hiram shouts the lyrics of a Tasked song he remembers from Lockless. Suddenly, there is a blue light and "the woods folding back against themselves" (148). Hiram sees Lockless on the day that Maynard made the Tasked run races; he sees his younger self fall and longs to comfort that little boy. The vision of the past fades and he returns to the present, but not to the place where he had been. Pain makes standing, even crawling, impossible. One of the hunters stands over him – but it is not who he thought; it is Hawkins telling him to make less noise.

Analysis:
The story of Maynard's selfish humiliation of the black slaves at Lockless, and his unthinking inclusion of his half-brother among them, is a reality that makes all claims following Maynard's death that Maynard loved Hiram nonsense. It also shows how tenaciously Hiram held onto the fantasy that, because of his birth and his obvious intelligence, he was of a different social status than the other Tasked.

The behavior of the man who owns him is strange. On the one hand, he treats Hiram like an animal by silently throwing him scraps of bread, but on the other hand the bread is wrapped in paper and he has arranged a table and chairs in the middle of the forest for them to sit at. This symbolizes the cultured veneer that hides the ugly reality of slavery.

There seems to be only two white men in the wagon so the black men outnumber their guards, but these blacks (including Hiram) are psychologically "broken"; Hiram feels himself "so tumbled in the pit of despair ... [that] I had been reduced to an animal. Now came the hunt" (141). One of the ways in which slaves were kept from contemplating any form of rebellion was the severity of the punishment for those who did so, and the hunt is an example of this since it is a 'game' that can have only one ending. Giving the 'criminal' blacks to Low whites to punish is a "brutality [that] was the offering Quality made to the low whites, the payment that united them" (142). Notice how these poorly dressed and uncouth Lows play like the Quality before their victims – how they pretend to be gentlemen.

Hiram runs as he ran when Maynard ordered him to, because he has no choice. Nevertheless, running is in itself a liberating activity. Ironically what the whites do to Hiram makes him stronger, faster, more cunning and more determined to avoid them, and also forces him to reflect on how to generate Conduction. It seems that the desire for freedom is a human right that not even the most brutal oppression can make men and women give up.

Hiram's third experience of Conduction shows the saving power of memory. He has reconnected with memories of his mother, and the slave song reminds him of his own past and the history of his people. This, in connection with the water of the pool into which he falls, triggers his power to cross time and space. It saves him from the Low, as it once saved him from death in the River Goose.

Chapter XII

Notes:

"'by Gabriel's Ghost'" (157): Gabriel, sometimes called Gabriel Prosser (1776-1800), was a literate enslaved blacksmith who planned a large slave rebellion in the Richmond area in the summer of 1800.

Guiding Questions:

48. In what ways is the speech and conduct of Corrine and Hawkins totally surprising to Hiram?

49. Explain why Corrine and Hawkins have allowed Hiram to endure the pit and the hunt rather than release him from those tortures as they had the power to? How do you feel about their motives?

50. Corrine insists that Hiram is not experiencing freedom. Is he?

Summary:

Hiram opens his eyes and sees bright daylight. He is in bed, washed and wearing luxurious night clothes. Only the pain in his ankle convinces him he has not gone to heaven. Hawkins and Corrine are present, but they act very strangely. Corinne smiles *at* Hiram, and there is, "nothing masterful ... no dominance in her manner, only a deep pleasure" that he is conscious. When he respectfully calls her, "'Miss Corrine,'" she corrects him, "'Corrine. Only ever Corrine'" (151). Hawkins is not standing by her as a serving man should but is seated in a chair beside Corrine. He tells Hiram, "'We're sorry,'" implying that he, "a tasking man, had some power here." Hawkins seems to be apologizing not just for the bump on Hiram's head but for all that he has experienced in the pit and the hunt. He says, enigmatically, "'Had to be sure ... Had some notions, but to be sure, had to carry you off'" (152).

Corrine insists that they must be totally honest with each other. She explains that, whether Hiram meant to kill Maynard or not, Maynard's death destroyed deep-laid plans. Corrine lights a tobacco pipe, and she and Hawkins pass it between them. Suddenly, Hiram realizes that the public image Corrine has cultivated "was a lie, the whole thing was a lie, the tradition. The mourning, perhaps even the marriage itself" (153).

Corrine identifies herself as a member of the Underground and tells Hiram that she has not acted only for his benefit, but "'we have long seen in you something of incredible value, some artifact of a lost world, a weapon that might turn the tide in this longest war,'" by which she means the "'war against unfreedom'" (155). She is speaking of the power that allowed Hiram to escape Goose River – the same power Santi Bess used to save forty-eight people by taking them down into the water.

Hiram is understandably confused, for it seems that Corrine and Hawkins have orchestrated all of his suffering. He asks where Sophia is, but Corrine indicates that they were powerless to save her. Hiram's anger explodes but Corrine explains they had to be sure he had the power of Conduction, and now they know he does. They suspected Hiram might be conducted back to Lockless, the only home he has ever know, and had agents waiting for him there. She promises that Hiram will understand everything in time: he is no longer a slave, but he will serve the abolitionist cause.

Analysis:

Hiram is pretty confused during the events recorded in this chapter; one senses that there are still parts of what happened that even the mature narrator does not know and/or does not fully understand. As a result, readers may find this a difficult chapter. Reading it twice might help. However, simply accepting that some things in life are beyond a full explanation may also help.

The behavior of Corrine and Hawkins is not just unconventional, it is revolutionary: they break every Virginian social norm in a matter of minutes! Corrine not only treats the story of Santi Bess as cold fact, she says she is "'convinced that the most degraded field-hand … knew more of the world than any overstuffed, forth-holding American philosophe.'" Corrine speaks of her gospel of freedom with the fervency of a religious convert. She calls the dance and song of the African people in America, "'an unwritten library stuffed with a knowledge of this tragic world, such that it defies language itself'" (153). This is the voice of a true believer.

The exact role that Corrine and Hawkins played in Hiram's arrest and punishment is not clear. It seems that they did not control Georgie Parks and therefore he was responsible for Hiram's arrest, and that of Sophia. However, they certainly wanted Hiram put through the test of the pit and the hunt because only in this way could they create the circumstances that would result in an act of Conduction. Whether this was managed, or they just let it happen, we do not know. They certainly knew where Hiram was and made no effort to rescue him. What they would have done had no act of Conduction occurred, we can only speculate.

The actions, past, present and proposed, of Corrine and Hawkins raise the old ethical problem of means and ends. We have already seen that the Quality will use any means, no matter how cruel and brutal, in order to maintain the position that slavery gives them. However, Corrine and Hawkins seem, in turn, willing go to the same extremes in their crusade to bring down slavery. Tricking Howell and Maynard into a sham marriage is one thing, but allowing Hiram to be tortured day after day in order to confirm his super power, when as his legal owner she could presumably at any time have repossessed him from the Virginia gentlemen and sacrificing the innocent Sophia, is quite another. Now, although Corrine insists that Hiram is free, telling him, "'You are not a slave. Not to your father. Not to me. Not to anyone'" (155), it is clear that she regards him as subject to "'a new binding, and in this binding – in this high duty – you will find your true nature'" (157). She and Hawkins may prove to be as ruthless as any enslaver.

It is worth adding, however, that the continued uncertainties of Hiram's position and of his future (we still do not even know where he is) is a real motivation to read on.

Chapter XIII

Notes:
"'or threaten a seven and nine'" (162): I have been unable to trace this reference which is used several times in the novel.
"German '48ers" (163): After the failed Revolution of 1848, in which the thirty-nine German states sought democracy and increased political freedoms, thousands of German revolutionaries fled Europe and emigrated to the United States.

Guiding Questions:
51. Identify the stages in the training that Hiram receives at Bryceton.
52. What doubts about the Virginia Underground and his place in it continue as Hiram learns more? How does he plan to resolve his doubts and fears?

Summary:
Later that day, Hiram smells cooking and comes downstairs to find Corrine, Hawkins, Amy, Mr. Fields, and three unknown blacks sitting down to dinner. Corrine invites him to join them. He partakes of, "the most indulgent meal" he has ever had and afterward everyone joins in to clear and remake the table. Hiram is shocked because, "There was no division" such as he has been raised to expect (159). In the parlor, they play blind man's bluff – spirits are high in celebration of Hiram's recovery.

Next day, Hiram sleeps late, luxuriating in the luxury. Seated alone on the veranda, he concludes that this must by Bryceton, Corrine's estate. Two white people appear from the woods; the younger nods, but the older pulls him back into the woods. Hiram sleeps and his dreams are an amalgam of his recent experiences. Amy wakes him. She tells him, "'there are thing about this place, about this new life, that you should know'" (160). She confirms that they are at Bryceton, which Corrine inherited and has made into a station of the Underground Railroad. Amy and Hawkins were once owned by the "'meanest man in the world,'" who married Corrine, but now is dead (162). Amy explains the different kinds of agents including the field agents, like herself, who have the dangerous role of going onto plantations and leading the Tasked to freedom.

By day, Hiram works on crafting furniture, but after dinner he joins in the training regime: he runs six or seven miles in an hour, then studies with Mr. Fields, and finally browses through the library. There he starts to write down his thoughts and experiences – the origin of the book we are reading.

After a month, Hiram comes to Mr. Fields for his lesson but finds Corrine waiting. She tells him that her fight for freedom for the Tasked comes out of her awareness of the subjection to which women have been held, "'since the days of Rome'" (166). Corrine hands him a package containing documents (letters, authorizations, and bills of sale) which belong to an enslaver and must soon be returned. She gives Hiram a week to become totally familiar with this man's life and psychology. After that period has elapsed, Corrine questions him exhaustively on every detail of the enslaver's life. Finally, she instructs Hiram to produce documents in the enslaver's hand relating to his favorite jockey, Levity Williams who will need, "'a day-pass for the road, a letter of introduction ... and ... free papers signed by his master" (168). Hiram forges the papers, and though he never finds out if they free Levity Williams, Corrine continues to bring him packets of documents and he produces forgeries to subvert the power of the enslavers: "Every soul sent to freedom was a blow against them" (169). His nights are still troubled by dreams.

Hiram learns of an Underground agent named Moses who also has the power of Conduction. She, however, has control of her power though she refuses to share the secret with the Virginia Underground. Corrine and the other top agents experiment with Hiram in attempts to induce Conduction, but nothing happens. Despite these failures, Hiram feels "[f]or the first time in my life, I was aligned with the world around me," and this makes him happy (171).

Talking with Corrine prompts a darker thought: he knows far too much about the Virginia Underground "ever to be released back into the world" (171). He was not brought to Bryceton because of his education but for his power. She desperately needs him to learn to control that power because Conduction destroys distance so they can free people in the Deep South. Hiram asks what will happen to him if he is unable to control Conduction, and Corrine replies that he is free. This seems to Hiram like another of her evasions, for he clearly serves as she directs. Angrily, he asks to take part in saving people. He wants proof that the Virginia Underground is not as unreal as the pretense Corrine used to deceive the Virginia Quality.

Analysis:

Bryceton is a kind of utopia, the very antithesis of Lockless. Amy certainly conveys the joy she feels every moment in being free to do what she wants. The organization that Amy describes is multifaceted. Corrine has been able to build it only because she inherited the estate and its wealth from her late husband. Bryceton is not, however, the alternative world that the Tasked inhabit in the swamps. Bryceton is not an end in itself; it exists only to enable the Tasked to make their way North to the free states. Everyone on the estate sees themselves as a warrior fighting a just war.

As Amy's words make clear, the Underground is not the swamp world that Hiram imagined; it is not a place at all. Rather, it is a network of people covertly working to free people from slavery. However, even so soon, Hiram makes a distinction between the other agents and himself. He sees them as "zealots" willing to do whatever the war needs – like the whites who supervise the physical training, some of whom he is convinced only recently hunted him. He writes, "their war was against the Task, and mine would be a war for those who were Tasked" (164). Corrine is leading a fight against an institution; Hiram wants to lead a fight for the victims of that institution – there is a huge difference. The question persists in the reader's mind whether Corrine is simply exploiting Hiram.

Corrine is an abolitionist because she is a feminist: her empathy for the Tasked originates in her awareness of the way in which women are systematically denied the rights of man. Women are "'told that knowledge is rightfully beyond us, and ornamental should be our whole aspiration ... The mind of woman is weak – that was the word'" (166). Her rebellion has not merely taken the form of attaining knowledge that men have sought to keep from her, but using that very knowledge to bring down patriarchy. Similarly, Hiram's intelligence was fostered by Howell in order to equip him better to serve Maynard; that is, it was used to support the institution of slavery, but now that same education makes him a valuable asset against the Quality.

One inevitable consequence of researching the enslavers whose documents Corrine brings, is that Hiram learns the intimate details of their lives so that these enslavers become human to him. Indeed, he admits that "[t]heir humanity wounded" him, because their concerns are the same concerns he has felt. He even finds in the documents, "a grim understanding of the sin of the Task." Almost, he loves them, but still he uses what he has learned to "strike out and destroy them (169).

There is much that disturbs Hiram about Corrine. He wonders what happens to agents who "revealed themselves to be liabilities" (171). From what he knows of her, he has no doubt that Corrine would have them killed, and that means that he will never be able to leave the organization despite what she tells him about being free. He even wonders if the Virginia Underground actually does free any of the Tasked. Perhaps it is just another of Corrine's deceptions.

Chapter XIV

Notes:
"a grift" (178): i.e., a petty or small-scale swindle.
"pokeweed" (180): Pokeweed, poke sallet, or poke salad, is a poisonous perennial plant which, properly prepared, is a nutritious food.

Guiding Questions:
53. Compare and contrast the views of Hiram and Corrine on taking revenge against Georgie.
54. Why does Hiram initially question the Underground decision to rescue Parnel Johns?
55. Lucy has done some pretty selfish things. What are they? How does she justify her behavior to Hiram?

Summary:
To allow Hiram "into the deepest sanctums of the Underground," Corrine needs to be sure he can never leave and to guarantee this, she demands "the destruction of Georgie Parks" (174). He cannot be murdered because that would arouse suspicion, so he must be implicated in betraying the enslavers and aiding the Underground. This will result in terrible vengeance against him and his family. With some reluctance, Hiram agrees.

A month later, Hawkins and Fields tell Hiram that their mission is to liberate Parnel Johns, a Tasked man who has been stealing from his master and selling to the Low. Unable to locate the thief, the master has punished all the slaves on his plantation causing them to turn against Johns who wants out – desperately. He is "'something of a genius'" who plays the violin. Hiram questions whether Johns deserves freedom, but Hawkins insists, "'It isn't about freedom. It's about war.'" Hiram, he says, must stop thinking and trust in the "'higher plan'" (179). To help Hiram to trust, Fields reveals that his real name is Micajah Bland, so Hiram now has information that could get Bland killed.

The three walk south-east for six hours. Johns is at the rendezvous, with his forged documents but accompanied, contrary to the agreement, by his seventeen-year-old 'daughter', Lucy. Hawkins is angry, but Fields persuades him to take them both. They walk for hours before sleeping by day in a cave. While Hiram is on lookout, Lucy admits that she is the lover not the daughter of Johns, who has a wife and children on the plantation. She explains that she pressured Johns to bring her because she could no longer tolerate life as a slave. After more walking, they reach a safehouse cabin where they leave Johns and Lucy with an old white woman – the next conductor on the railroad North.

Four months after his arrival at Bryceton. Corrine and the others decide that Hiram should go to Philadelphia. He is given papers identifying him as Hiram Walker, a free black, and he travels with Bland and Hawkins (in the role of Bland's enslaved servant). As the train pulls out, Hiram tells himself, "*I am free*" (186).

The Water Dancer by Ta-Nehisi Coates

Analysis:

The plan to get revenge against Georgie shows some of the contradictions of the Underground that Hiram now serves. Though he has dreamed of revenge against Georgie, Hiram's "wrath faded in the face of the full shape of what must necessarily follow," by which he means the fate of Amber and her baby (174). Corrine is certainly right about the scale of Georgie's crimes and the unutterable suffering to which he has condemned others, but Hiram finds the clear logic of Corrine's conclusions chilling. Georgie was, like everyone else, trapped in the institution of slavery – he was also a victim. By what right does Corrine condemn him? Hiram realizes that the war against the Task is "not the ancient and honorable kind" (176). The fight against a merciless enemy must be waged mercilessly.

When it comes to freeing Parnel Johns, Hiram continues to think in term of individuals, but Hawkins and Fields urge him not to seek to understand everything the Underground does but to trust in the grand plan. Hawkins tells him that the aim is not to bring justice to the Tasked (there are simply too many of them) but to bring justice to the masters (of whom there are fewer and whose fall will bring down the system). After they have picked up the cargo (Johns and Lucy), Hiram knows that if there is any sign of slave hunters on their trail the cargo will be killed because the agents "could not risk any word getting out about our methods" (181).

Johns is a thief and is unfaithful to his wife; Lucy is concerned only with her own freedom. Hiram finds himself condemning both of them, but Lucy will have none of it. To Lucy the concepts of right and wrong are irrelevant in the context of "'what they did to us back there'" (183). In such a system, everyone has to look out for themselves, and that is what she intends to do. After all, she is merely following the example of her beautiful, cruel young mistress who ran off with the preacher because she wanted to see the world. Ruthlessness operates on both sides. Hawkins warns Johns that if he ever tells of his escape then the Underground will kill him.

Hiram at last gets to call himself Walker, his father's name, but a name he was denied by his illegitimacy and his color. It is also an ironically appropriate name since Hiram is now free to walk wherever he wants, which as a Tasked man he was not. Symbolically, the surname makes him the white man's equal.

The decision to remove Hiram to Philadelphia "to see more of the Underground's work" comes as a surprise to Hiram (184). That is acceptable. However, it also comes as a complete surprise to the reader, and that may not be fine since moving him seems more to do with the author's desire to expand his protagonist's experience than with genuine motivation. Presumably the plan to get revenge on Georgie has been put on hold.

Chapter XV

Notes:
"Clarksburg" (187): Clarksburg is the county seat of Harrison County, West Virginia.
"a lady keeps her clutch" (188): A clutch is a small, often elegant, woman's bag or purse.
"Gray's Ferry Station ... the Schuylkill River" (188): Near the ferry and later bridge over the Schuylkill River in Philadelphia.
"cinched waist" (189): A dress that pinches in the waist to produce an hour-glass figure.

Guiding Questions:
56. What surprises Hiram most about the status of blacks in Philadelphia?
57. What exactly happens to Hiram after he bites into the gingerbread while sitting on the bench by the river?

Summary:
Hiram, Hawkins and Bland all plan to take the same circuitous route to Philadelphia in order to avoid Ryland's Hounds, but Hiram travels separately from the other two. He boards a train that does not have a separate "'nigger car'" because, "The Quality kept their Tasked ones close the way a lady keeps her clutch, closer even ..." (188). After two days, they get off the train at Gray's Ferry. A well-dressed black man introduces himself to Hiram as Raymond White, and they ride an omnibus. Everything he sees is new to Hiram who notes that "the rich were mostly white and the poor mostly black, but there were also members of both tribes in both classes" (189). Clearly whites hold the power here, but they do not hold it exclusively. He sees black people dressed more elegantly than any of the Virginia Quality, yet paradoxically the city stinks – literally!

Raymond takes him to a house where his brother Otha White is drinking coffee with Bland and Hawkins. Hawkins tells the brothers to take care of Hiram, whom he calls "'the genuine article'" which Hiram calls "the kindest thing Hawkins had ever said to me" (191). Otha seems to have been born in slavery down South while Raymond was born free up North. Hawkins tells them they will have to teach Hiram everything and then says goodbye, adding that they will probably never see each other again. Otha shows Hiram his bedroom, and they have dinner at a local tavern. Otha lives in the same house as Hiram, whereas Raymond lives outside the city with his family.

Hiram wakes before seven next morning to walk around the city. He continues to be dazzled. Entering a bakery, the proprietor, a black man, introduces himself as Mars, the cousin of the White brothers, which, he says, makes Hiram family. Hiram is suspicious of the man's openness, which later he regrets. He leaves with the gift of a piece of hot gingerbread.

Beside the river, he sits down on a bench to unwrap and eat the gingerbread.

The Water Dancer by Ta-Nehisi Coates

It occurs to Hiram that "this was the freest I had ever been in my life": there is absolutely nothing to stop him from abandoning the Underground and disappearing into the city (194). However, his first bite plunges him into a memory: he is a child in the kitchen at Lockless watching a black woman whose name he cannot recall make gingerbread for Maynard. Knowing he craves some, she surreptitiously gives him two pieces saying, "'Family got to watch out for each other … And furthermost, as I see it, all of this belongs to you anyway ... Don't forget … Family'" (195). The memory dissolves, and when he comes to himself, Hiram finds he has teleported three benches down the promenade.

Analysis:

It is ironic that the train Hiram boards does not have a segregated car for blacks. Black travelers are so infrequent that there is no need. The result is that trains are integrated in ways that they would not be again in the South until the post-Civil Rights Era.

Everything about Philadelphia is strange to Hiram. Above all, life has taught him to be suspicious of everyone, yet here there seems to be an openness and trust between people that he has never known.

This scene where Hiram bites into the gingerbread is the author's act of homage to one of the most famous moments in literature. Marcel Proust's *In Search of Lost Time* (1871–1922) [alternative translation *Remembrance of Things Past*] begins when the taste of a madeleine (a traditional French cake) dipped in tea inspires an involuntary memory of the narrator's childhood.

Chapter XVI

Guiding Question:
58. What does this chapter add to your understanding of the way in which slavery robs the Tasked of the pleasures of family?

Summary:

His spontaneous Conduction leaves Hiram exhausted, and he goes back to bed. Next morning, Saturday, Otha calls on him to accompany himself and Raymond. Raymond explains that state law guarantees that an enslaved person who claims haven must be granted their freedom, but he also says that masters keep the law secret or tell their slaves lies, and that it is illegal for anyone to prompt a slave to ask for their freedom. The three board a riverboat that is shortly going to cast off and go downriver. Here they find a well-dressed black woman, Mary Bronson, with a small boy. She is a slave, brought North by her master, who has made a request regarding her freedom; the White brothers intend to enforce her legal rights. The white owner angrily states, "'I mean to return with my property to my home country,'" but Raymond points out that he is not *in* his home country, and the crowd takes the side of Mary and her little son (199). Mary ignores the master's threats, and the man literally appears to shrink as he realizes his helplessness. The boat leaves the pier with the frustrated enslaver on it.

Mary and her son are taken back to Otha's house where they are given a meal. It is the custom of the station to record the stories of those who are enfranchised, and Raymond insists on this because "he believed himself in the midst of history and felt strongly that all pertaining events should be well recorded" (201). Mary says her son is was called Octavius, adding, "'Ol massa decided that like he decided everything else'" (201). Mary has a husband and two other sons down South. She is a skilled cook, and her first master hired her out and shared her wages with her. She planned to earn enough to buy her own freedom and then the freedom of her other family members, but the old master died and the new owner (the man on the boat) not only ended that arrangement but sold her husband and two elder sons, and began beating her. Mary cries and Otha compassionately comforts her. He promises that she and Octavius will be looked after, but Mary insists that she will not be free until she is reunited with her family. Her words remind Hiram of his own losses: his mother, Thena, and Sophia.

Hiram begins working three days a week in a woodworking shop and three days for the Underground. Otha invites him to dinner at his mother's house to meet the family. Ironically, in the countryside, Hiram feels some nostalgia for the South, for though the institution of slavery is repugnant, that is still his home. As he approaches the house, the evident love and affection radiating from it takes him imaginatively back to the Street, and he experiences a "reunion with a mother I could not remember" such as he felt in the River Goose, though no teleportation results (206).

The house is full of family members. Surrounded by a love that is founded on security, Hiram begins to let go of the natural caution and suspicion that life at Lockless has bred into him. After dinner, one of the girls plays the piano, and the pride of the whole family is evident. Hiram thinks sadly about generations of enslaved children, including himself, whose genius has been stolen from them. Afterwards, Otha tells Hiram the complex and sad history of his family. Otha and his brother Lambert were left in slavery after first his father and then his mother (Viola) escaped North. The brothers were sold South as punishment for their mother's flight. Lambert died a slave and Otha escaped but had to leave his wife, Lydia, and their three children still enslaved. For a long time, Otha felt "'a low heavy hatred'" for his mother, Viola, but in Philadelphia he met his brother Raymond, an agent of the Underground, who was able to reunite Otha with his mother (209). Otha now understands that Viola did the only thing she could; like Mary Bronson, he knows the sorrow of a broken family.

Analysis:

In Virginia, the laws support the right of enslavers to do as they wish with their property. Slaves have no legal redress, and though free black people do in theory have such redress, the law does not regard them as equal with even Low whites. In the North, however, the Underground agents are protected by state law, so long as they themselves do not break that law. The white man tells Raymond, "'Boy … If I were home I'd have you in your proper place, and break you good,'" but Raymond is not intimidated (200). He is a man whose legal standing is equal with that of the enslaver and who knows that in this case he has the law on his side. The enslaver has no experience of a black man speaking back to him and is out of his depth. We learn nothing of the racial composition of the small crowd that gathers, but it is likely to be multi-racial. Its sympathies are entirely with the enslaved woman.

The Underground understands the importance of recording the narratives of freed slaves. Down South, the Tasked have an oral culture with stories passed by word of mouth from generation to generation, but up North their stories are written down as the stories of whites have always been. Mary's testimony reminds the reader of the limitations of the Underground. She obviously feels guilty at having abandoned her husband and sons, and cannot regard herself as free while they remain enslaved. Otha is honest enough to admit that the Underground does not have the power to save them, to which Mary replies, "'If you can't stop them from breaking us up … if you can't put us back together, then your freedom is thin and your church and your city hold nothing for me'" (204). What Mary demands would take a civil war.

Neither the Bronson nor the White families can ever be truly whole because loved family members remain enslaved in the South, beyond the power of the Underground to redeem. The Tasked have to make the terrible choice between freedom and family. Mary finally makes that choice. When Viola ran, she tried to explain to Lambert and Otha that she could not take them with her, "'Cause I can only carry so many, and them only so far'" (211). Otha himself made the same heartbreaking choice, leaving Lydia and their two girls.

Chapter XVII

Guiding Questions:

59. Explain the difference between the conception of freedom that leads Hiram to attempt to walk away from the Underground and the conception of freedom that he develops after being rescued from the man-catchers.

60. How does Bland justify not preventing Hiram from being taken and killing his captors in cold blood?

61. On what grounds do Raymond and Otha object to the way Corrine used Hiram and Sophia? Where does Bland now stand on this issue?

Summary:

Hiram experiences Conduction more often. He begins to piece together his memories and feels that "something was trying to reveal itself," but each experience leaves him "with a somehow deeper sense of loss than the one I'd carried into it" (212). He decides to walk away from the Underground, but when night falls, he realizes he has, "no plan ... really had no way out, no way to escape the Underground nor the binds of memory" (213). He decides to return, but is approached by a white man, struck on the head and passes out.

When Hiram regains consciousness, he is chained, blindfolded, and gagged in the back of a moving cart. He knows he has been kidnapped by Ryland's Hounds of the North who will sell him into slavery. A girl next to him is crying. As his abductors eat around a campfire, shots are fired. Hiram, another black man and his daughter are freed by Micajah Bland. Hiram vents his fury on the corpses of the dead whites until he is too exhausted to kick anymore. Hiram realizes that Virginia bred in him a desire for freedom only "for me and those I chose," but now he must dedicate himself to freedom for everyone because all of the Tasked are family (116). On the road, Bland meets a small woman a little older that Hiram: this is his first encounter with Moses (aka The General, The Night, The Vanisher, Moses of the Shore) – she whom Corrine called "the living master of Conduction" (217).

Bland tells Hiram he was watched, and when the men took him, he followed and shot them to "'make their cohort understand the perils of their trade'" and thereby save others from being taken (218). Hiram talks of his love for Sophia and how he feels that he failed her. Bland explains that the pain Hiram feels now is "'the feeling that marks an entire nation held down'" (219). Hiram's pain is not his alone.

The next morning, Raymond, Otha and Bland are waiting downstairs for Hiram. Raymond tells him that, though he trusts Bland completely, he does not approve of some of his actions when working for other stations such as that run by Corrinne. Specifically, Raymond disapproves of how Hiram and Sophia were treated. Bland joins in the apology and tells Hiram that he knows where Sophia is: Corrine persuaded Howell to take her back. Virginia station rules dictate that she be left there, but Otha and Raymond say that they have different rules: they "'know precisely how to bring her out'" (221).

A Study Guide

Analysis:

This chapter focuses on the concept of freedom. Hiram believes the sailors are "the most free" because they are men without ties to other people, free to come and go as they want (213). In contrast, Hiram feels tied to the Underground. In their work songs, sailors remind him of the Tasked, but these men sail across the water by their own choice, not like the slaves brought from Africa who could only achieve freedom in death by jumping overboard.

Hiram's rage against the man-catchers is not personal. It is, "the rage of everything from my mother to Maynard to Sophia to Corrine, all the lies, all the violation…" (215). He understands that the voice inside him that told him to flee Lockless is the same that told him to flee the Underground; it represents a selfish desire for his own individual freedom. After all of his experiences, he feels it to have been replaced by a commitment to family – the family of the Tasked. He is now finally ready to use the personal freedom he has achieved in the service of others.

Bland's killing of the man-catchers raises again the question of ends and means. Hiram is shocked that the Underground watched him be taken and did not intervene. Bland replies that it was necessary because the men could only be shot in the open country, not in the city. To Hiram the shooting is murder, which technically it was since Bland did not give the men any warning. However, Bland answers that if being a murderer is what it takes to save more people from being taken South and sold into slavery, then he will accept the name. To Bland, as to Corrine, "'This work, this war … gives my own life meaning'" (219) – or to put it another way, the end justifies the means. However, the Railroad is not a single, coherent organization, but rather a confederacy of groups with different aims and values. To Raymond, using people as Corrine used Hiram and Sophia wrongs the cause. Bland understands that stations operating in the South take a more ruthless, pragmatic approach than those in the North; nevertheless, in Hiram's case he agrees with the White brothers that the means discredited the end. He wants to right a wrong.

Chapter XVIII

Notes:
"'Box' Brown ... Ellen Craft ... Jarm Logue" (226): Henry Box Brown (c.1815-1897) was a Virginia slave who, in 1849 at the age of thirty-three, escaped by having himself mailed in a wooden crate to abolitionists in Philadelphia. Ellen Craft (1826-1891) and William Craft (1824-1900) were slaves from Macon, Georgia who escaped in December 1848. Ellen posed as a white planter and William as her personal servant, and together they traveled openly by train and steamboat. Rev. Jermain Wesley Loguen, born Jarm Logue, (1813-1872) escaped slavery at the age of twenty-one using the Underground Railway.

Guiding Questions:
62. What mistake has Hiram made in relation to Sophia's liberation?
63. Bland admits that Corrine has done things of which he, Raymond, Otha and even Moses would not approve. Why does he not condemn her? What is the most ruthless thing that Hiram suspects her of having done?

Summary:
Hiram obsesses on the idea of Sophia coming to Philadelphia and the life they might have together. Two weeks later, Raymond invites him to his home where he shows Hiram crates of papers documenting almost every rescue by the Philadelphia Underground. Raymond says that Hiram deserves a chance to be reunited with Sophia and that Bland is going to handle it personally. The station is, however, also working on rescuing Otha's wife Lydia from Alabama, and Bland must complete that mission first. Hiram says that he understands, "'Everyone – but everyone in their time'" (225).

Raymond says Bland needs help to get to Alabama in good time, but the mission is so dangerous and it is personal rather than Underground business. Sophia, he promises, will be rescued whatever Hiram decides. Hiram agrees to do it and smiles his first "open generous smile, one that rose out of a feeling with which I was rarely acquainted – joy" (225). Hiram spends hours reading the documents, which really bring to life for him the heroism of the escapees and those who help them. He eats dinner with Raymond's family and stays the night.

The next day, Hiram walks to Bland's house. He is understandably nervous, particularly of Low whites. For the first time, he really notices the poor blacks in the city, mostly runaways who are isolated because they have rejected support from the Underground and belong to no church.

Bland's house is more modest than that of either of the White brothers. His sister, Laura, answers the door. Hiram talks of their two missions. Bland is confident that he can persuade Corrine to help rescue Sophia, but Hiram objects. He feels himself possessed by anger at Corrine for having left Sophia at Lockless. It is not just personal anger but that of a whole people, and it brings on the blue light of Conduction. This time Hiram is aware of what is happening and tries to control the power but soon finds himself back in the room with Bland, though the two have somehow changed places.

Later as Hiram walks with Bland, he asks why Moses, who has the power to control her power of Conduction, does not go down South to save Lydia, but Bland explains that Moses, "'has her own promises to keep'" – once again, the scale of the crime is too great for any one person to deal with (231). Bland explains how he met Corrine while she was attending a finishing school in New York. She was recruited, the Underground seeing a Virginia gentlewoman as an ideal agent to take the war into the South. He admits that she has done things (he says, she has made "'[t]remendous sacrifices'"), that others would never approve of, but asks Hiram to consider what would happen to her if she were ever unmasked (232).

Analysis:

Hiram comes to understand that the demands upon the Underground are much greater than its resources, both in terms of money and agents. Understandably, his priority is being reunited with Sophia, but the fact is that almost everyone in the Underground has relatives whom they want rescued. Hiram sums up what he has learned when he tells Raymond that in Philadelphia he has seen, "'what we are fighting for … all that is coming'" (225). Hiram understands the importance of the slave narratives that he reads: these stories of real suffering and great heroism really bring home the realities of slavery.

The fate of poor blacks in Philadelphia illustrates that physical freedom is just the beginning of a process. Without support, freed slaves do not have the economic or the social skills to thrive in a city.

Hiram has already hinted that, in seeking to escape with Sophia he was thinking of his own version of freedom and ignoring that Sophia might have her own "*dreams*" and her own concept of "*redemption*" (229). The mature narrator reflects sadly that he, "who so prided himself on listening, simply could not hear" what she had said to him before they tried to escape (229). This foreshadowing suggests that Sophia will assert her own vision of the life she wants, and that it will not necessarily include Hiram.

Just how ruthless has Corinne been? Hiram shares with Bland his suspicion that she murdered her own husband to secure her inheritance. Bland makes no comment – which might be seen as an admission.

Chapter XIX

Notes:

"Benjamin Rush" (236): Rush (1746-1813) was one of the Founding Fathers. He signed the United States Declaration of Independence and represented Pennsylvania in the Continental Congress. During the Philadelphia yellow fever epidemics in 1793, 1794, and 1797, Rush treated his patients by purging the body via bloodletting and vomiting – treatments that only made them weaker. Rush also believed that blacks were immune from the fever and that the African American community's assistance with this epidemic would help them to win allies in their quest for greater freedom – he was wrong on both counts. He became a convinced abolitionist in later life.

"the Seminole War" (237): There were three wars between the United States and the Seminole Indians of Florida (1817–18, 1835–42, 1855–58). Bland must have fought in the second of these.

Guiding Question:

64. What factors make freeing Lydia such a difficult and dangerous enterprise?

Summary:

That night, Hiram realizes that, at present, he is the victim of his Conduction. Since the only person he knows who controls Conduction is Moses, he concludes that he will have to speak to her. But first there is the matter of freeing Lydia.

Next day, he, Bland, Otha, and Raymond discuss the plans. Lydia is owned by Daniel McKiernan, and to forge passes for the Underground agents, Hiram needs a sample of the man's handwriting. It is known that he does business with one Elon Simpson, the son of the man who once owned the White family, who owns a house in Philadelphia. At night, Bland takes Hiram to Washington Square, a rich white neighborhood literally built on the mass grave of slaves who died of fever in the days when slavery was still legal in Pennsylvania. Here Simpson has a house.

While they watch, Hiram asks Bland how he came to the Underground. Bland explains that his experience as a young man in the Seminole War, and the terrible atrocities he witnessed against Native Americans, put his own problems of poverty and lack of education into perspective. Eventually, he found the cause of abolition.

A white man comes out of the house and hands Bland a package of documents. Bland insists on going into the house to check that the documents are what he needs, but the man (evidently Simpson's servant) objects. Bland threatens to tell his master of the affair the man is having with Simpson's sister, and he capitulates. The papers prove useless, but Hiram finds in Simpson's chest his correspondence with McKiernan, "records of transactions – records of people managed, bought, and sold" (240). They take what Hiram needs to forge the passes in McKiernan's name.

A short time later, Bland leaves for Alabama on "the most daring rescue anyone in Philadelphia had ever undertaken" (241). Bland's route is circuitous and complex, and it is August, so the nights are not long. However, McKiernan is said to be in financial trouble which means he might sell off slaves at any time.

Analysis:

The account of the tragic history of Washington Square allows the author to remind the reader that the anti-slavery position of the Northern States is relatively recent. There was a time when slavery was legal throughout the American Colonies and subsequently the United States. Hiram comments, "even here, in the free North, the luxuries of this world were built right on top of us" (237). The name of Dr, Rush is revered in American history because of his part in the American Revolution. However, the use that he made of black people is neither medically sound (since they died in great numbers) nor in accordance with the principles for which the American Revolution was fought.

Elon Simpson is a respected man in Philadelphia and mixes in the highest circles of its society, "But shut away in that foot-locker was his unwashed life – the proof of a great crime, evidence of his membership of the dark society that underwrote his opulent house" (240). Just as his Washington Square house is built on the bodies of dead slaves, so his current wealth is maintained by ownership of the bodies of slaves. The locked chest in which he keeps his slavery correspondence is a fitting symbol of his shameful, hidden life.

Chapter XX

Notes:

"the Knight and the Whistle" (247): A version of Hunt the Whistle, a child's game. The hunter is made a knight. During this process the whistle is secretly attached to his/her coat. The knight then tries to find which of the other children has the whistle. To confuse the knight, the others surreptitiously blow the whistle until the knight makes the discovery that he has had the whistle all along.

"not merely to improve the world, but to remake it" (252): Compare, "We have it in our power to begin the world over again" (Thomas Paine appendix to *Common Sense*, 1776)

Guiding Question:

65. By the end of this chapter, Hiram has come to see the struggle against slavery in a wider social context. Explain the conclusion he has reached.

Summary:

Raymond, Otha, and Hiram drive in a hired coach to the annual abolitionist convention in New York State, the only time when agents of the Underground meet with those working openly to end slavery by changing the law. Moses, whom Raymond calls Harriet, joins them. Hiram calls her, "a soul scarred but not broken, by the worst of slavery" (243).

Walking through the convention campsite near the Canadian border, Hiram hears orators promoting a wide range of "[n]ew ways of being, new ideas of liberation" – abolition of alcohol, equal rights for women, rights for native peoples, an end to child labor, the right to unionize, communal living, and free love. To Hiram it is, "an entire university out on the green" (245).

A woman a little older than himself approaches Hiram and introduces herself as Kessiah, Thena's daughter, with whom Rose used to leave Hiram as an infant. Hiram is stunned, so Kessiah does most of the talking. She recounts her relatively happy childhood which ended when her father, Big John, died of fever, and Thena was devastated by her grief. Hiram does manage to tell Kessiah that Thena was good to him, adding, "'For me, Thena was the best part of Lockless'" (249).

Kessiah tells of how she and her siblings were separated and sold by Howell, so she never saw any family members again. Enslaved in Maryland, Kessiah met a freeman, Elias, who began working toward buying her freedom. When Kessiah came up to be sold at auction, Elias drove up the price and appeared to lose out to a man from Texas, but Moses saved Kessiah. She has been with her ever since and recently heard rumors about a slave who had escaped from Lockless. Kessiah hugs Hiram warmly and he responds. She asks how Mamma Rose is doing.

That night, black people around a campfire sing, "the songs that could only be made down in the coffin [i.e. Southern slavery]" (251). The day has been momentous for Hiram. He now sees, "Slavery was the root of all struggle" in the sense that the Task is only one way in which free people are enslaved. Thus, the secret war he is fighting is, "against something more than the Taskmasters of Virginia"; it involves remaking the world (252).

A messenger hands Hiram a letter from Bland. He takes it to Otha and Raymond: it states that Bland has Lydia and the children, and they are currently in Indiana.

Analysis:

Taking his protagonist to the New York convention does allow the author to relate slavery to other issues of human bondage, but it also seems a little arbitrary – something done more for the ideas than as a consequence of plot or character.

Kessiah and Hiram's reunion "seemed incredible" to Hiram, and the reader may feel the same (247). However, the author gives it a semblance of plausibility: the Underground is a relatively small network that efficiently communicates. Kessiah's story is yet another way of bringing home to the reader both the ways in which slavery tears families apart and the ways in which its victims form improvised familial structures to compensate for what has been taken away from them. There is a further point, however, for slavery does not lose its power to pull people apart once an individual achieve freedom. We have already seen several cases of slaves leaving wives, husbands and children in slavery when they decide to escape. In Kessiah's case, following her freedom, she decided to follow Moses because the work of the Underground seemed to her more important than her personal "pains" (250). Her husband had to learn to accept this.

Chapter XXI

Notes:
"a seven and nine" (259): I wish I knew!

Guiding Question:
66. Explain why Lydia is so essential to Otha's happiness.

Summary:
On the evening on the second day, walking high in the hills, Hiram comes across Moses sitting alone. on a rock. She tells him of her work and of her dream of eventually living openly and freely in her home in Maryland. Hiram brings up his frustration with Conduction, but Harriet just tells him to, "'Give it time.'" She confides that she has a particular job where she needs, "'a man who runs least as well as he writes'" (254). Hiram is surprised since he knows that Moses usually works alone, but he agrees enthusiastically. She tells him they will start soon, but nothing more.

Next morning, Hiram is woken by a commotion. Leaving his tent, he sees the normally calm Otha weeping on Raymond's shoulder, hysterical with grief. Otha shouts that Bland has been killed and Lydia returned to her owner. Hiram confirms details of the story by reading the papers in the satchel that had brought the news to Otha. He returns the papers to Raymond, who is seated with Otha (now calmer) and the leaders of the Underground, including Harriet and Corrine Quinn. He leaves.

Hours later, Otha comes to Hiram's tent. Otha unburdens himself to Hiram because he knows that Hiram has suffered the same separation from someone he loves. Otha calls Bland his brother, whom he loved. He tells Hiram that, despite his sorrows at the loss of those he loved, he has "'never, for an instant, shied away from connection, from love'" (258). Knowing how Hiram is struggling to control his power of Conduction, he tells him his own story.

Otha met Lydia shortly after Lambert's death. From the depths of despair, Lydia taught him to laugh again. They were to get married, but days before the wedding, Otha found Lydia in a great deal of pain. The headman had made sexual advances that she had resisted, and he had whipped her. Otha swore to kill him, but Lydia, knowing that Otha would be killed in revenge, stopped him. She told him, "*This is not our end … This is not how you and me die*'" (260). This message saved Otha, and he obviously wants Hiram to take it to heart. Otha stands and vows, "'My Lydia will be free'" (260).

Analysis:
It finally occurs to Hiram that his youthful wish to inherit Lockless in the place of Maynard was no more than a dream "of ruling, as my father had done" (253).

The Underground Railroad fails sometimes. The novel has already stressed that, despite the bravery and (occasionally) the ruthlessness, of its agents, when they are operating in the slave states everything is stacked against them. The description of the brutal murder of Bland illustrates the vengeance that whites will take against 'race traitors' (we remember what Bland had earlier told Hiram of the fate that Corrine Quinn would suffer were she ever to be exposed). Nevertheless, Otha's moving statement that Bland, "'was not my blood, but he was so much my brother that he would die for me and mine,'" restores the reader's faith that the racial divide is artificial and can be transcended (258). Otha's determination not to give into defeat, to believe that the story is not supposed to end with people in slavery, is just what Hiram needs. Despite the progress he has made in understanding the struggle, Hiram still has a tendency to see everything as it relates to him personally; he needs to be reminded of the bigger picture.

Chapter XXII

Guiding Question:

67. Contrast the attitudes of Hawkins and Hiram to Bland's failure and death.

Summary:

When the convention is over, they all travel together in three carriages: Hiram, Raymond and Otha; Harriet and Kessiah; and Corrine, Hawkins, and Amy. Knowing how much Bland meant to Hiram, Kessiah expresses her condolences; Hiram feels "drawn into her. She was the elder sister I had never thought to need, the plug in the hole that I had not even known was there" (262).

That night, Hiram wakes from a dream that begins with Maynard drowning in the Goose and the blue light he experienced, but ends with Bland being the one who drowns. The thought strikes Hiram for the first time that it was the papers that he forged that got Bland caught, and he feels tremendous guilt. Walking outside, Hiram finds Hawkins, Amy, and Corrine smoking cigars together and sharing their tender memories of Bland. Hiram joins them and says he was to blame for Bland's capture. However, Hawkins and Amy insist that it was not the papers that Hiram forged but the sickness of one of the children that caused the whites to suspect that Lydia and the children were runaways. Bland was not immediately arrested, but his evident interest in them eventually led to his arrest. It was a risk he knowingly took.

Analysis:

The Underground agents Corrine, Hawkins, and Amy deal with the failure of the escape plan and Bland's death in different ways. The one thing that unites them is the determination that this failure will not stop the war. Corrine remembers how Bland saved her by showing her, "'a world that I had not even glimpsed'" – a thought that Hiram echoes (263). Hawkins and Amy know how dangerous an escape attempt in Alabama was, but Hawkins is angry that it was even attempted, and all "'for some babies'" (265). Hiram understands that this anger is Hawkins's way of dealing with the tragedy. He himself understands that the babies were Otha's, and that the Underground is about more than mathematical calculation. He concludes, "I knew this was part of the work, to accept the losses. But I would not accept them all" (266).

Chapter XXIII

Notes:

"'Poplar Neck – Dorchester, Maryland'" (269): Poplar Neck plantation was owned by Anthony C. Thompson. From here, Tubman led her three brothers, Robert, Henry, and Ben, Ben's fiancé Jane Kane, and their friends John Chase and Peter Jackson to freedom on Christmas Day, 1854.

"'Beacon Hill, Boston'" (269): A famous landmark in Boston.

"'Hampton's Mark … Elias Creek'" (275): I can find no places by these names.

Guiding Question:

68. Finally, the narrative describes a full and successful act of Conduction. What more do you learn about what is necessary to enable Harriet and Hiram to slip through space/time?

Summary:

Back in Philadelphia, Hiram's life returns to routine, and he sees Kessiah regularly. However, the Underground makes necessary operational changes in the light of Bland's capture.

Early in October, Harriet meets him. She tells him that Underground agents are involved in a war, and that people like Bland are ready to sacrifice their lives because they, "'cannot bear to live in the world the way it is'" (268). Harriet discusses their mission to Maryland for which she needs him to produce passes for two people, and tells him to send to Jake Jackson a letter written by an enslaved person that contains a special signal. She concludes that they will set off in two weeks and that the journey will take one night, which leaves Hiram confused, because that, "'Ain't enough time to get to Maryland'" (270). Harriet only smiles enigmatically.

Two weeks later, Hiram meets Harriet at the docks in the middle of the night. She leads the way down a pier telling Hiram, "'memory is the chariot, and memory is the way, and memory is the bridge from the curse of slavery to the boon of freedom.'" Hiram realizes that they are walking over the water, exploiting the power of Harriet's "chain of memory" which is so powerful that images appear of those whom she remembers (271). She tells Hiram of her childhood as a slave, beaten repeatedly by her mistress until she almost thought that was, "'God's plan,'" and that she was, "'the wretch they made me out to be, and deserved no more than the abuses I received'" (272). She recalls how she was sent to trap varmints in the swamps at only seven years old and tells him of Abe, whom she calls "'our boy'" (273), an orphan whose mother died in childhood and whose father had been sold long before. He was a freedom-loving rebel, always running away when the whites tried to punish him, and always too quick for them.

Hiram is "gripped by her telling," and it is this power that Conducts him. Harriet tells of one pursuit of Abe when, in total frustration, the slaver old Galloway threw a weight at the young slave that hit her and knocked her unconscious, in which state she had a vision of an army of Abes in blue uniforms descending on the "'sinful country'" singing a battle hymn. Harriet tells how she was in a coma for four months, and once she awoke had months of recovery, but in her head, she never afterwards doubted the victory over slavery. From Abe, Harriet learned, "'the first feeling of what it might mean to be free'" (275). She tells Hiram that she heard Abe had finally been captured but does not believe it. In a way this is true, for Abe, like all of the others who are lost and gone, lives free in her memory.

Hiram realizes that they are no longer in Philadelphia, "A door had opened. The land had folded like fabric. Conduction. Conduction. Conduction" (276). He hears the horn calling the Tasked to their labor in the fields. On the negative side, Harriet has collapsed because of the strain.

Analysis:

So, having returned to Philadelphia, Hiram does not think to visit Laura, Bland's sister, whom he knows, to console her? Either that, or he simply does not record having done so. Both seem equally unlikely.

To Harriet, the death of agents in the war on slavery is inevitable. Tomorrow it might be Hiram, or herself. She is more stoical than Hawkins: death is preferable to a life under a system that makes living unendurable.

Finally, the author gives a detailed depiction of Conduction. However, the narrator can only describe the experience as he perceived it then. Do not look for a scientific explanation that makes everything clear; look for an evocative description of what it *felt* like. Harriet does, however, stress three factors that we already know to be essential to Conduction: the evocation of memory, dancing and the presence of water. Readers will have different views on how effective this description is, as they will on how appropriate it is to give a historical personage a super power that they demonstrably did not have.

Harriet's vision of an army of Abes in blue uniforms descending on the "'sinful country'" singing a battle hymn proves to be prophetic for that is exactly what will happen to the South during the Civil War when the Union Army, the army of Abraham Lincoln, defeated the Army of the Confederacy (275).

Chapter XXIV

Notes:

"Harriet really had pulled the pistol on the coward" (284): One of the legends surrounding Harriet Tubman is that, when she was conducting some slaves to freedom, one of the men took fright and tried to return to the plantation. Harriet pointed a gun at him and said, "You go on or die." Once a rescue is begun, "'*none shall turn back*'" (284).

Guiding Questions:

69. How is the power of Conduction linked right back to Africa?
70. What lies has Robert told Mary in the past? Why has he planned to abandon her? Why does he change those plans?

Summary:

The sun is rising on Maryland, but Hiram knows they are not safe here. There is always the danger of slave hunters, and even the Tasked working in the fields might be tempted to turn them in for the reward. Hiram carries the unconscious Harriet to the woods and finds her a secure hiding place. After a day spent completely hidden still deeper in the woods, Hiram returns to Harriet who appears completely recovered. She explains that Conduction works through memory, "'on the strength of our remembrances, we are moved,'" but that the strain of remembering can be debilitation (278). She adds that she has made this jump many times and has no idea why this one taxed her so.

Harriet leads to a cabin in the woods which is their destination, but first she tells Hiram to ask any questions he has now because there will not be time later. Hiram tells her about his grandmother, Santi Bess, a pure-blood African with a talent for storytelling. One day, Bess told her daughter, Rose, that she was going where Rose could not follow. That night, she walked down to the river in the middle of winter and disappeared, along with forty-eight of the Tasked, all pure-bloods like her. Hiram says he has never known how to feel about that story, because both his grandfather and his mother were left out of the disappearance and were sold down South. He asks point blank how Harriet, and by extension Santi Bess, achieves Conduction.

Harriet uses the image of islands in a river. Most people have to swim from island to island, but some people perceive bridges which are composed of stories of the past of the African peoples. Captives on slave ships dove into the water and were conducted back to Africa. Now, however, the black slaves have been so long in America that "'we have forgotten the old songs and lost so many of our stories'" (280). Hiram admits that he has lost all memory of his mother. Harriet suggests that part of him is repressing those memories and that he needs, "'something outside of yourself ... a lever to unlock that thing you done shut away'" (281).

Harriet stresses how long it took her to "'regulate the power'" she had following her extended coma (281-282). She does, however, point out that the common element in Hiram's experiences of Conduction is water: each time, he was metaphorically standing at the ramp of a bridge to another island. Hiram is amazed not to have seen this link. He asks why Harriet did not use her Conduction power go to Alabama to save Lydia, and she explains that she cannot travel to places of which she has no memory, nor can she conduct strangers.

Inside, Harriet introduces Chase Piers, the owner of the cabin; her brothers, Ben and Henry; and Henry's wife, Jane, whose head has been shaved to enable her to pass for a man. Harriet is in complete control, and everyone is relaxed because they have faith in her, "She was the only agent never to fail at a single rescue, never to lose a passenger on the rail" (284). Another brother, Robert, is with his wife who is about to give birth, and Hiram's task will be to fetch him. Hiram walks to the plantation where, about sunrise, he locates Robert and tells him to be at the same place at night. When Hiram returns, Robert does not appear. With the example of Bland before him, Hiram refuses to leave Robert behind, so he goes into his cabin where he finds Mary accusing Robert of lying about going to see his family and planning to run off to a social with the Jennings girl.

Hiram intervenes telling Mary the truth: Robert is about to be sold and is escaping. He identifies himself as Robert's conductor and promises, "'we will not rest until you and your Robert are brought into reunion'" (290). Mary moans the same way Sophia did when she and Hiram were captured. Hiram tells her his name, and vows to get Robert out safely. Mary acquiesces, and Robert kisses her goodbye.

On their way to the rendezvous, Robert tells Hiram that Mary is pregnant not by him but by the son of her enslaver. He is angry at her for not having prevented the white man from taking advantage of her (though in truth she was completely powerless to do so) and cannot tolerate the idea of raising another man's child. His plan was to leave Mary and start a new life alone in the North, but hearing what Hiram said reminded him that he really does love her. However, Robert expresses bitterness that enslaved people have nothing pure. In reply, Hiram points out that white people have nothing pure either, but *they* fool themselves into believing that they do.

Analysis:

Here Harriet experiences exhaustion after Conduction, just as Hiram always has. Memory is power, but remembering can also be very painful. Freud would talk about the dangers to psychic health of repressed emotions and the liberating effect of releasing those emotions. Something similar is happening here, although the liberation triggers a paranormal event.

Strangely, Hiram only now tells all that he knows of the story of his grandmother, Santi Bess. The story has come up several times in the narrative, and he has given no indication of knowing what he now tells Harriet. Most importantly, we learn that Santi and those whom she Conducted to Africa were pure-bloods (i.e., having only African ancestry). The African blood of the Tasked has become diluted as the first generation of imported slaves has been succeeded by blacks born in America and also by mixing with the blood of whites. Conduction, then, is a spiritual power related to African ancestry.

Perhaps what the author means is not physical pure-blood so much as a metaphor for culture. Certainly, in being abducted and transported to America, black people lost their identity – not immediately, but inevitably. The old religions died, the old customs fell out of use, and the oral histories were forgotten. If taken literally, the concept of pure-blood is problematic since it is so often used to support the idea of racial purity – white separatists use it all of the time. Genetically speaking, there is no validity in the concept of human beings being divided into races. The concept of pure blood also seems to contradict what Hiram says about the virtue of accepting that nothing in life is pure. Readers must make their own way through this minefield.

Yet again, we get an explanation of Conduction. There is a great deal of repetition in all of this, though a few new elements are added each time. The fact is that, if the reader is a rationalist who, like Hiram, feels "the whole [of human experience is] explicable, comprehensible through books," then no amount of explanation will convince (279). If the reader believes, with Hamlet, that, "There are more things in heaven and earth … Than are dreamed of in your philosophy" (*Hamlet* Act 1 Scene 5), then explanation is really unnecessary.

The author avoids one obvious trap in a novel that takes sides against slavery: his Tasked characters are flawed and imperfect human beings (with perhaps the solitary exception of Harriet). Robert has been unfaithful to Mary, and he has lied to her about his plans to escape both slavery and her in the North. He is also guilty of double standards: he has himself been unfaithful to Mary, yet he feels that, "'raising some other man's baby, it grind on a man in a kinda way…'" (293). His sexism here reminds us of Hiram's earlier awareness that freeing people from slavery is only part of freeing them from other ways in which their liberty and dignity is stolen.

The final discussion between Hiram and Robert is interesting. Robert sees that the Tasked get nothing pure: the part-white baby Mary is carrying is a painful symbol of this. Hiram, however, knows that whites get nothing pure either: they have to enslave their own children (as he himself was enslaved by Howell). The difference is that the owners pretend that they are pure; they deny the reality that is staring them in the face, which makes them hypocrites. In contrast, black people are honest; they know, "'Ain't no pure … Ain't no clean'" (293). Once, Hiram aspired to be of the Quality, the self-blinded, but now he would choose to live among the honest oppressed.

This is fair enough, but how does it relate to the concept of the pure-blood African still in touch with his/her roots and with the mystical power of Conduction? Since the blacks forcibly brought across the Atlantic were from different, often warring, tribes, how does it make sense to talk of their pure blood? The author seems to be trying to have it both ways.

Chapter XXV

Guiding Questions:
71. Why is Ma Rit not told of the escape? Why does Pop Ross wear a blindfold?
72. What do we learn of Harriet's relationship with and feelings toward John Tubman?

Summary:
Harriet's parents are free, and it is in their stable that the runaways gather. However, Ma Rit is kept ignorant of their presence because, if she knew her children were leaving, she would become emotional, and if she were later questioned about their disappearance, she would not be able to lie. Harriet, who has been free ten years, has been back several times, but has never seen her mother. For the same reason, the father, Pop Ross, takes extravagant measures not to actually see any of the fugitives so that, if asked, he can honestly say he has not seen them. When Hiram brings Robert, Harriet hugs him tightly. They wait for Ma Rit to go to sleep, and when Pop Ross comes out to speak to them, he is wearing a blindfold.

In the night, when Ma Rit is asleep, Jane and Henry lead the blindfolded Pop Ross to the pond. On the bank, Harriet says goodbye and kisses him; the green light of Conduction emanates from her hand, illuminating Pop Ross's tears. Harriet dedicates the journey to John Tubman (her husband), Pop Ross, and Ma Rit, three people whom she loves but has had to leave behind. She tells about her life and the others act as a chorus enhancing the memories.

Analysis:
The theme of family separation is given a new dimension. Here, free parents have children who are not free. (In fact, Ben Ross, was freed in 1840 at the age of forty-five by the will of his former master, Anthony Thomson, but the rest of the family remained enslaved). If the enslaved children decide to run, they have to leave their parents. Not only that, but in order to protect their parents, they have to keep their plans secret from them. In securing her own freedom, Harriet was forced to abandon her husband, John Tubman, and when she returned for him, she was no longer the same person and he was living with another woman. She is not bitter, however, praying for him, "'May you find a love that love you, even in these shackled times'" (300).

Chapter XXVI

Notes:

"The Kidnapped and the Ransomed" (305-306): The reference to Otha's book reminds us that slave narratives were an important way of educating readers on the evils of slavery in America and of raising funds to support the abolitionist cause. Coates has in mind the 1856 narrative of the same title by Peter and Vina Still, which recounts their separate escapes from the South and subsequent reunion in the North. "From the mid-1820s, writers consciously chose the autobiographical form to generate enthusiasms for the abolitionist movement. Some writers adopted literary techniques, including the use of fictionalized dialogue. Between 1835 and 1865 more than 80 such narratives were published. Recurrent features include: slave auctions, the break-up of families, and frequently two accounts of escapes, one of which is successful" One of the earliest was *Life of William Grimes, the Runaway Slave* by William Grimes, published in 1825. (Wikipedia contributors. "Slave narrative." *Wikipedia, The Free Encyclopedia*. Wikipedia, The Free Encyclopedia, 4 Jan. 2020. Web. 4 Jan. 2020).

Guiding Question:

73. Hiram believes that he has found the key to recovering his memory of his mother and thus to controlling his power of Conduction. Explain what he has come to understand about his memories.

Summary:

Before dawn next morning the group materializes at Delaware Avenue Docks in Philadelphia where Otha and Kessiah are waiting by prior arrangement in a storehouse. Harriet is again exhausted. Seeing Kessiah, Hiram becomes emotional because he understands now that she is his, "bridge back to Virginia," to Thena and Rose (302). He realizes that he forgot his mother because of his own dreams of inheriting Lockless from his father Howell, the savior who would raise him out of slavery so that he, in turn, could save Lockless. Now that he has finally discarded that old self-deception, he is a better person. He is embarrassed to be crying in Kessiah's arms until he sees that the whole group are holding each other and crying.

At Otha's house, they all have breakfast. Robert tells Hiram that he needs Mary, and Hiram promises to speak to Harriet since it was him who promised that the Underground would come back for her. Raymond hands Hiram a letter from Corrine Quinn calling him back to the Virginia station. Though Raymond insists that he owns nobody anything, Hiram feels himself "to truly be on the Underground, and besides he is determined to free Sophia" (304). When he tells Harriet of his decision, she predicts that he will soon learn to control his power of Conduction but warns him not to, "'let them pull you into their schemings'"; that is, not to allow Corrine to exploit his power for her own ends (305). She tells him to contact her through Kessiah if he ever needs her help.

The Water Dancer by Ta-Nehisi Coates

The next day, Hiram finds Otha, Raymond, and Kessiah talking in the dining room about their plans to get Lydia and the children out. McKiernan wants to sell them; they are in contact with him via an intermediary. Kessiah shows Hiram a book called *The Kidnapped and the Ransomed*, Otha's account of his escape from slavery. The plan is to sell the book around the North, thereby raising the money to buy Lydia and the kids. Buying the freedom of slaves is not the way the Underground normally works, but for Otha it is the only way. Hiram tells them he will be returning to Virginia and tries haltingly to explain how knowing them has changed him. Otha embraces him and says, "'We know'" (306).

Analysis:

The chapter begins, "And there we were early the next morning ..." (301). This is perhaps an unfortunate choice of words. It sounds a little too much like, 'And with one tremendous bound he was free!' Describing teleportation in a convincing way is certainly not easy, but this opening is frankly a little lame.

Throughout the novel, Hiram has struggled to understand why he cannot remember anything about his mother, Rose. Now, suddenly, he gets it: his pursuit of the illusion of a benevolent father who would see that he inherited Lockless has actually led him to betray his mother, and to hide that betrayal from himself, he has repressed all memory of her. He writes that he, "went off into the house of Lockless like I had no mother," but now he is, "shedding the lie, like an old skin" (302).

When Hiram first joined the Underground, it was hardly a free choice. In effect, he had changed one master (Howell) for another (Corrine). That is, however, no longer the case. Now he is making a free choice to return to Virginia: he does not *have* to walk away from the Underground anymore because he knows that he *is free* to walk away from the Underground but he chooses not to do so. (This is a paradox that is used several times in the novel: it is why Sophia finally commits herself both to Hiram and to staying in Elm County as a slave.)

Chapter XXVII

Guiding Question:
74. What pressure does Corrine put on Hiram in order to persuade him to return to Lockless as Howell's manservant?

Summary:
Hiram walks with Kessiah one last time before leaving Philadelphia. Recent events have left them both emotional. Kessiah finds it hard constantly to leave her husband in order to do her work for the Underground. Hiram promises to bring Thena up North. Kessiah says she would love to see her mother again and set her up on the farm that she and her husband own.

The next morning, Hiram's Philadelphia 'family' escorts him to the railway station, and he notices (but does not communicate with) the white Underground agent who will shadow him and intervene in the case of trouble. As he travels South, Hiram feels slavery as, "a weight beyond anything I had ever known" because in Philadelphia he has experienced freedom. Back at Bryceton, he vows that he "never wanted to again breathe free air" while Sophia and Thena are still "in chains" (311). He knows it will be difficult to persuade Corrine to free Sophia and Thena: Sophia because, as Nathaniel Walker's personal property, he will take revenge against the Underground, and Thena because the Underground concentrates on freeing young people.

Corrine tells Hiram that, in causing Maynard's death, he saved her from having to endure a horrible marriage, but that her plans to infiltrate the elite of Elm County in the interest of the Underground also died with Maynard. She tells him that Roscoe, Howell's manservant, has died and that Howell wants Hiram to take his place. (Remember that Corrine bought Hiram from Howell following Maynard's death.) She asks Hiram to accept because it will allow him to gather information about Lockless Plantation, and he immediately does so on condition that Corrine agrees to free Sophia and Thena. When he insists, she concedes.

The next day, Hiram puts on the clothes of a Tasked man and travels with Corrine, who still wears mourning, though her gown is more elaborate and she looks every inch Virginia Quality. They drive to Starfall, where Hiram sees evident signs of economic decline and growing decay. Entering an inn, Hiram sees ten Low whites drinking silently, but when Corrine gives the secret words, he is amazed to find them all to be Underground agents and himself to be in the secret Starfall station. With nothing else to do that day, Hiram wanders over to Freetown – or rather to where Freetown had once stood. Georgie's house has been burned to the ground and everything destroyed; this is how the Underground got its revenge for his betrayal of Hiram and other escaping slaves. All he finds is the toy horse he once carved for Georgie's baby which he puts in his pocket.

Analysis:
The Underground Railroad appears not to differentiate based on the gender of

its agents. Harriet, Kessiah, Corrine, and Amy perform roles normally reserved for men and take risks from which men would normally protect women. To Kessiah it gives the independence she has always wanted; she loves her husband but is not dependent upon him. For his part, he has to learn to accept that she is away from home a great deal.

Corrine continues to manipulate Hiram. For example, she asks if he has made any progress in gaining control over his powers of Conduction, but wisely Hiram keeps silent. She pressures him into going back to Lockless as Howell's manservant by reminding him that all of her plans were ruined when Maynard died. However, Hiram is more than a match for her. He now has his own demands and is confident of attaining them. He tells her, "'I am not the same man. I know what this war means, and I am with you in it. But I cannot rescue on a symbol. They are my family, all the family I have ever had. And I want them out'" (314). Corrine is incapable of such feelings for family, while Hiram is bringing what he learned about family in Philadelphia back to Virginia.

In establishing a station at Starfall, Corrine has achieved something remarkable. She is undoubtedly a brilliant agent even though she tends to fight the war on her own terms, which makes her sometimes out of step with the mainstream Underground. How convincing Corrine is as a character is an open question. It really does seem that too many people know of her double life for it to remain a secret as long as it does.

The fate of Georgie, and even more so of his wife and family, raises again the issue of ends and means. The Underground has punished Georgie for the people he has already betrayed and taken effective action to prevent him betraying others, but the collateral damage is significant. Hiram writes that seeing, "the harvest of the Underground's terrible revenge, which had not merely vented itself on Georgie Parks but on the entirety of Freetown," he "felt a deep and pervading shame" (317).

PART THREE

Chapter XXVIII

Notes:

"Tuscaloosa" (331): In west central Alabama was the state capital from 1826 to 1846 (when it was relocated to Montgomery).

"Cairo" (331): The county seat of Grady County, in south west Georgia.

Guiding Question:

75. Analyze Hiram's reaction to his reunion with Sophia.

Summary:

Next afternoon, Hiram drives over to Lockless, avoiding the stone bridge where Maynard died. He describes himself as "drowning in a bleed of feelings" as a result of seeing his father again, of the shame of his parting words to Thena, and of reuniting with Sophia, but more than all these having "a deep-seated and boyish hope that the decay ... [that] had overrun Elm County had somehow spared my Lockless" (321). However, in the year he has been absent, Lockless has indeed shrunken into decay, and when he sees his father "he seemed to have aged ten [years]" (323).

Hiram greets his sleeping father with formal politeness, but Howell runs to embrace him, crying, and repeatedly calling him, "'My boy'" (322). Howell evidently thinks that Hiram has been working at Bryceton since Corrine persuaded him to transfer ownership to her. He asks Hiram how he feels about coming back to Lockless, and Hiram says it strikes him very well. Howell tells Hiram to find something better to wear amongst Maynard's clothes. He says that Lockless is changed, that he needs Hiram to oversee the running of the plantation, and that in his old age he has become very concerned with finding a suitable heir. He says he regrets two things in his life: having sold Rose to Natchez and having sold Hiram to Corrine.

Hiram finds only two elderly slaves working in the kitchen "which itself said something of the straits Lockless now navigated" (325). Hiram serves dinner and takes a drink to Howell in his study. Going down into the Warrens to his old room, he understands better than ever before "the whole dimensions of the crime [of slavery], the entirety of the theft ... so that men such as my father might live as gods" (325).

He hears Thena humming in the room next to his own, but when he approaches, she continues with her sewing, ignoring him. He makes a full-hearted apology for the way he had left her, telling Thena that she is, "'all the family I have, more family than anyone who has ever lived in this house'" (326). Finally, Thena squeezes Hiram's hand, and he knows how much she loves him. He gathers some of his old things, takes them to his new room, and puts Howell to bed.

Next day, Hiram brings Corrine, Amy, and Hawkins over for a visit. After they leave, Hiram serves Howell supper and goes down to see Thena. He notes again how empty and quiet the Warrens are. They eat supper, and Thena asks if Hiram has seen Sophia. He replies that he assumed she would be over at Nathaniel's place, but Thena replies that Nathaniel is mostly in Tennessee. Corrine has made some kind of "'arrangement'" whereby Sophia is largely left "'to her business … Till they figure out what to do with her'" (329).

On Sunday afternoon, Hiram walks to the Street to visit Sophia. Although the cabins have also fallen into disrepair, he finds her living in the cabin that Hiram and Thena used to share. Sophia is holding a baby. She tells Hiram that she is called Caroline (Carrie) and that she is not his; from the baby's color, Hiram knows that Nathaniel is the father. Hiram is conflicted: part of him wants, "to get away from Sophia, to never speak to her again" because she is no longer *his* Sophia, but the part of him educated by his experiences in Philadelphia is "shocked to find such resentment still curdling in me" (332). Speaking of the people who have been sold off, Sophia says, "'They are killing us all,'" but she sees Hiram's return to her, his second return from the dead, as having, "'Some powerful, powerful meaning'" (333).

Later that evening, Hiram tell Thena that Sophia must have been pregnant when she escaped with him, and that she ran with him because of the pregnancy. He resents the fact that he was completely honest with Sophia but she was not with him. Thena tells him that neither Sophia nor her has heard the full story about why Hiram ran away because "'ain't nobody straight down no line'" (334).

Analysis:

Howell calls himself, "'a conflicted man,'" but "'a new one [too]'" (324). Both descriptions apply equally to Hiram who loves both Lockless and his father despite the fact that both are inextricably linked with the institution of slavery that he hates. Hiram admits the contradictions in his feelings, but understands that humans are emotionally complex and that feelings are not rational. He concludes, "I was what I was and could no more choose my family, even a family denied me, that I could choose a country that denies us all the same" (321). Similarly, part of Howell has always loved Hiram as his son. Hiram sees in this now the same joy he "glimpsed all those years ago when I'd caught the rotating coin…" (323). However, Howell has, until now, been prevented by the relationship imposed between them by slavery from ever acknowledging his feelings, even to himself. The way that he now speaks of Roscoe shows his affection and respect for his old servant, but Roscoe still died his slave. His dressing of Hiram in Maynard's clothes, giving him Maynard's room, and handing over the management of Lockless to him indicates that he now sees his mixed-race son as a suitable heir, something he was prevented from doing by the barriers of race. Similarly, he speaks of the mistake of "'letting go'" of Rose and Hiram, when he actually sold them, as he had done to many others before and since, separating them from their families (324).

Thena has lost everyone she ever loved: her husband to the fever and her children to the auction block. When Hiram left Lockless, however, he chose to do so, which must have made his desertion all the more bitter for her. Nevertheless, she loves him. She, also, is a complex, conflicted human being.

Corrine has evidently not told Hiram that Sophia is back at Lockless, though it is not clear why. It might, for example, have been a strong incentive for Hiram to accept the idea of returning to the plantation as Howell's servant. In some unspecified way, Corrine has used her influence to separate Sophia from Nathaniel and to ensure that her position is safe, in the short term at least. Thena's reference to Sophia's "'business'" strikes the reader as needlessly vague, but all will soon be revealed (329).

When he sees the disrepair of the Street, Hiram once again meditates on the self-destructive nature of the institution of slavery. He reflects that, if the Quality had shown the same virtues of hard work and good land management that their ancestors had shown, then the ruination of the soil, and of the lifestyle its bounty supported, would not have happened, but that "the fall was always ordained, because slavery made men wasteful and profligate in sloth" (329). Having said that, in this final section of the novel we do not get any indication that Hiram actually does anything to manage the plantation more efficiently.

The reader now understands the mature narrator's earlier hints that Sophia had her own reasons for wanting to be free. Hiram's reaction to the baby mirrors that of Robert reacting to Mary's baby earlier, and ironically it is Thena giving the wise advice about the complexity of human motivations that Hiram then gave to Robert. Both men have to learn to overcome their selfish instincts to possess a woman, to make her *theirs* in the same way that slavery makes the Tasked the possessions of the Quality.

Chapter XXIX

Guiding Question:

76. Sophia uses a paradox to explain the only way in which she will become Hiram's wife, "'But what you must get is that for me to be yours, I must never be yours … I must never be any man's'" (345). Explain what she means.

Summary:

With few visitors other than Corrine, whom Howell still views as "the daughter he'd never had," Hiram is his father's sole companion (336). After dinner, they talk and drink together. Howell confides that his own father never loved him, and that he wanted Maynard "'to be what his own nature commanded'" (336). Howell now sees that he failed to prepare Maynard to the life of a plantation owner – indeed, he tells Hiram, "'I had hardly been built for it myself,'" though he always saw the necessary skills in Hiram (337). Howell confesses that he is "'not a "good man"'" and tells Hiram he has "'not forgotten what was done to you'" (337). This is the closest Howell will ever come to a full acknowledgement of his crimes, for he was raised as Quality who never have to apologize for anything. Howell drifts off to sleep. Hiram takes his cider into his father's study where he takes out the plantation ledgers documenting the financial problems of Lockless. Because this is the information Corrine wants him to get, he studies them until he has memorized the contents. While Hiram is taking Howell up to bed, Howell says, "'I got plans for you, boy. Plans'" (338). He then asks Hiram to tell him a story, and Hiram tells him an inspiring story of the founding of Lockless by "our progenitor" – note Hiram's use of the plural possessive pronoun (338).

Next day, Hawkins drives Corrine for a visit. Hiram walks Hawkins down to the Street and tells him that the ledgers he saw indicate that Lockless is deep in debt and that Nathaniel has advanced Howell a lot of money without getting any if it back. Hawkins tells him to keep an eye on the ledgers. Hiram has been avoiding Sophia, though he had hoped to see her in the Street. He still feels for her as he did a year ago, but it troubles him to know that "some part of my welfare was in the hands of someone who had her own secret motives and desires" (339).

Hiram learns that, with Howell's approval, Thena has started hiring herself out to do laundry for the local houses which have also sold off many of their slaves. With the money she makes, she plans to buy her freedom. Hiram drives Thena to pick up dirty laundry from her clients, and Sophia (with Carrie) comes along because she has been helping Thena. On the drive, Hiram cannot hide his sense of hurt at what he sees as Sophia's betrayal, and Sophia reminds him that she warned him she was never going to owned by a black husband the way she had been owned by a white master. She bitterly tells him he is, "'stewing over what you don't own, over what no man should ever try to own. You supposed to be better'" (343). Angrily she walks away.

After serving dinner, Hiram eats with Thena who tells him he is punishing Sophia. Having thought things through, he goes to find Sophia. He apologizes profusely, for everything he has put upon her. He takes her hand and promises that he is "'trying to be better'" (344). Sophia kisses his hand and tells him she understands that he wants her to be his, "'But what you must get is that for me to be yours, I must never be yours ... I must never be any man's'" (345). Hiram realizes that in all his fantasies about Sophia, he has never allowed her to be the woman she wants to be herself; she has been a substitute for the mother he lost and was helpless to save. Hiram gives Sophia the carved wooden horse for Carrie, saying, "'I am trying'" (345).

Analysis:

Howell acknowledges the injustices of Hiram's life without actually taking responsibility for having caused them or directly apologizing to him. Howell's regrets are sincere, but even now he cannot bring himself to face the enormity of the suffering that his behavior has caused. He is essentially a weak man. Since Hiram's return, Howell has consistently used the word 'boy' when addressing him. Speaking as father to son, 'boy' is a term of endearment, as when he greets Hiram with the joyous words, "'My boy'" (322). However, without the possessive pronoun, the word is a derogatory term typically used by a white (particularly an enslaver) to a black, as when Howell tells Hiram here, "'I got plans for you, boy. Plans'" (338). The narrative never clarifies exactly what these plans are.

Sophia knows that what Hiram cannot accept is the fact that Carrie is Nathaniel's daughter. She also knows that his dreams of having her as his wife define her as *his* in a way that takes from her the independence that she feels to be essential. It is to her credit that she challenges Hiram directly on both of these issues: she likes (perhaps loves) Hiram, but is simply not prepared to give herself to him. What she is prepared to do, however, is to give Hiram time to see whether he can overcome the need to be the dominant male in their relationship as he has overcome his desire to inherit and own Lockless.

Chapter XXX

Guiding Question:
77. This chapter will culminate in Hiram going to the River Goose and inducing an act of Conduction over which he feels, for the first time, he has control. What has he understood about the process of Conduction that makes this possible?

Summary:
Hiram, Thena, Sophia, and Carrie are the only Tasked at Lockless whom Howell will not sell: Hiram is his son, and Sophia and Carrie belong to his brother, and he feels the guilt of having sold all of Thena's children. Sophia and Hiram take over the collection and washing of laundry because, as Sophia points out, Thena is getting too old for the heavy work. One night when she is with Hiram, Sophia asks if he still has a problem with Carrie not being his child, and he tells her that it, "'Takes some adjusting,'" but that is precisely what he is trying to do (348). They talk about their running away and what happened subsequently. Sophia says she cannot understand Hiram's sudden disappearance, nor why she herself was not sold Natchez-way; she believes there is more to what happened than she knows. Hiram cannot tell her the truth, so he simply repeats his cover story about going to work for Corrine. Even he does not understand the interest that Corrine has taken in Sophia's well-being since her capture a year ago.

Looking at the baby, Hiram remembers what he learned about family in Philadelphia. He asks to hold Carrie and as he does so he reflects that Howell never held him, though he always wanted him to. He understands that Carrie, "'is not [my] blood ... 'Cept, she is my blood'" (350-351). As he once told Robert, it is mucky, but it now seems that he is determined to follow the advice he gave to Robert then.

Autumn is turning into winter while Lockless is, "hollowing itself out" (352). Carrie seems to be the one point of light in this world. Thena takes care of the baby while Hiram repairs Sophia's cabin. Having finished, they are both cold, so Hiram brings from his room a bottle of rum he was given in Philadelphia. This renews Sophia's suspicions. She says, "'I know there is something with you, something about the places you been ... You ain't the same man who left'" (352-353). To divert the conversation, Hiram asks what happened to Sophia after her capture. She tells him that her unborn baby, whom she would name after Carolina, the land from which she had been taken, gave her the strength to endue, and also that Corrine Quinn came to the jail, got her out, assured her that Nathaniel need never know, and returned her to Lockless. After that, Corrine visited regularly asking about the state of Lockless and telling her that he (Hiram) would return. Sophia tells him she cannot believe that Hiram came back to her because she has lost so much in her life. Hiram realizes how much he loves Sophia and that his love is returned. They make love.

Hiram feels "a new knowledge"; he feels the same love for Sophia as Otha feels for Lydia. This leads him finally to understand Conduction as, "a relay of feeling, assembled from moments so striking that they become real as stone and steel…" (356). With this knowledge, he gets dressed, and as he goes Sophia hands him the toy horse, saying that Caroline is too young for it anyway. Hiram walks to the River Goose where he experiences the first Conduction that he actually controls.

Analysis:

Hiram, Thena, Sophia, and Carrie form a three-generational family unit. They are tied both by blood (Sophia is Carrie's mother and Hiram is Carrie's cousin) and by emotional ties (Thena has long been Hiram's surrogate mother and seems to have the same relationship now with the adult Sophia). All of this is very impure and mucky, but that is the way life is for the Tasked through no fault of their own. Hiram has long understood that holding out for purity simply leads to ignoring the happiness that life *does* have to offer. The challenge that Hiram faces is the same as that faced by most Tasked people and many other characters in this narrative who have had to create ad hoc family units to replace the biological families that have been destroyed by slavery. Only by doing so can the Tasked ensure that the damage done by family separation is not passed to the next generation.

The detailed description of Sophia and Hiram doing a day's laundry brings home to the reader how laborious life was in these times. The simplest tasks took long hours of hard physical effort.

Sophia's account of Corrine's actions in releasing her from jail, protecting her from the consequences of Nathaniel learning of her attempt to escape, and reassuring her about Hiram's safety shows her in a much more positive light. Not only did her actions take a great deal of courage and planning, but they also provided Corrine with an inside source of information about the sale of slaves at Lockless. Nevertheless, she also appears to have been motivated by a genuine desire to help Sophia through a difficult period.

The rum that he shares with Sophia was given to Hiram in Philadelphia by Mars, the character who most represents the importance of family and who immediately extended that term to include Hiram to whom he was not related by blood. In sharing it with Sophia, Hiram is symbolically bringing to her all that he has learned since their arrest.

Chapter XXXI

Notes:

"Prophet Gabriel" (368): Gabriel Prosser (1776-1800) was a literate enslaved blacksmith who planned a large slave rebellion in the Richmond area in the summer of 1800. However, intelligence of the planned rising leaked to the authorities and he was arrested. Gabriel, his two brothers, and 23 other slaves were subsequently hanged.

"Nat Turner" (368): Nat Turner (1800-1831) was an enslaved African-American preacher who led a four-day rebellion in August 1831 of about seventy enslaved and free black people in Southampton County, Virginia. The rebellion caused the death of approximately 60 white men, women, and children. The state executed 56 slaves accused of participating in the rebellion, and approximately 120 slaves and free blacks were murdered by militias and mobs.

Guiding Questions:

78. What developments convince Hiram that Thena and Sophia must immediately be conducted to safety in the North?

79. What are Corrine's reasons for refusing immediately to conduct Thena and Sophia to freedom as Hiram wants?

80. Explain the "word-play" to which Hiram refers at the end of the chapter (373).

Summary:

The experience of Conduction leaves Hiram exhausted. For the next few weeks, he spends his nights with Sophia. They keep this development in their relationship a secret from everyone (though Thena perceives it) because they fear what Nathaniel Walker would do should he discover that *his* woman has been with a slave. In December, Nathaniel returns and Hiram has to drive Sophia to "their private business" as he has in the past (361). This is hard for Hiram, but he understands, "what was between us was not ownership, but a promise to be in the company of each other, by any means, for as long as we could" (359). On the way, Sophia tries again to get Hiram to tell her about his missing year. She says she knows that Corrine often travels North and assumes Hiram accompanied her. Hiram remains evasive and noncommittal.

Hiram asks how Sophia got to Nathaniel's while he was away. Sophia says that she was only called once and then she had to walk carrying all of her "'costume and effects'" (361). She describes her humiliation at having to change in the bushes and this leads her to express her hatred of white people and her fantasies of killing Nathaniel. When they arrive, a servant informs Sophia that Nathaniel, "'cannot have you today'" – note the double meaning of the word 'have' here (362). Both Sophia and Hiram are happy about this, and Sophia jokes that Hiram somehow arranged it. She adds, "'it is odd. I have never had it happen this way before'" (362). To reassure Hiram, she asserts that she has no wish to be back at Nathaniel's because, "'since you done come back, I feel myself to be as free as I have ever been'" (363). This is not the true freedom that she craves, but it is something of value nevertheless.

The mature narrator comments on how happy he was in this moment with "all the promises and tragedies ahead of me" (363). Hiram hints that there may be a way for them to escape the disaster that is inevitably overtaking Lockless, but Sophia is cautious since their last effort ended so disastrously. She tells him that before she will run again, she will need to "'know [the] how and ... [the] what'" (364).

When they return to Lockless, they find that Thena has a bandage around her head and that someone has broken into her lockbox and stollen the laundry money. Fortunately, Carrie is sleeping safely, and though she has no memory of the assault, Thena is not badly injured. Hiram concludes that the robber was one of the Tasked, but he has no idea who it might have been and sees no recourse even if he tells Howell. To be safer, Hiram, Sophia, and Thena all move into Thena's cabin on the Street, and they make sure Thena is never left alone. For the first time since he has known Thena, Hiram sees "true fear on her face, fear of what could happen remaining there at Lockless" (366). He concludes that it is time to make good his promise to Kessiah to bring her mother to Philadelphia. Shortly afterwards, Hiram learns from Howell that Nathaniel has planned to return from Tennessee but had been delayed by urgent business. Sophia shares with Hiram her fear that Nathaniel is planning to take her to Tennessee where, she has heard, white men take black women as their legal wives. She assures Hiram that she does not want that. This is another reason for Hiram to want to leave Lockless. He writes, "I felt it was time for Corrine Quinn to make good on her portion of the bargain" (368).

Corrine comes to stay at Lockless for the Christmas Holidays, bringing a great number of guests and servants filling the big house as in the old days, which makes Howell happy. It is, however, "a charade" for in reality all of them are Underground agents (368). Privately, Hiram explains the theft of Thena's savings and his fears that Nathaniel intends to take Sophia to Tennessee. He insists that Corrine must have Thena and Sophia conducted to freedom as she promised, telling her, "'I want them out. Both of them'" (371). However, Corrine counters that she has arranged with Nathaniel that, in one week, Sophia will become Corrine's property, so she is safe. She tells him, "'There are a great many things in the works, and we must take care to not endanger them'" (371). It suddenly occurs to Corrine that Hiram may have learned how to control the power of Conduction and thus have a way to free Sophia and Thena. She urges him not to "'doom us,'" by which she means those working for the Underground in Elm County, and Hiram relies, "'I promise not to doom us,'" but by this he means himself, Sophia and Thena (373).

Analysis:
The call for Sophia to be driven over to Nathaniel's reminds us of how powerless the Tasked are. The memory that once during the previous year she had

to walk over and change into her dress in the bushes shows how insensitive Nathaniel is to her feelings. Their being turned away on this occasion is, of course, positive in the short term, but it is also unprecedented and that foreshadows some unexpected development. Sophia's hate-filled rant against white owners in general and Nathaniel in particular is something new in the narrative. It shows the built-up frustration of one who is controlled both as a black person and as a woman: she is doubly helpless.

The conflict between Hiram and Corrine has several facets. Corrine sees the 'big picture' in the sense that she has plans against the institution of slavery in Virginia, though she remains typically uncommunicative about what these plans are. In contrast, Hiram acts out of personal feelings for the individuals whom he loves. This is what Corrine means when she urges him to, "'Think beyond your emotions. Think beyond all you guilt'" (372). To Corrine, the Tasked are weapons to be used in the war, while to Hiram they are "people with lives and stories and lineage" (368). Corrine acts out of hatred of slavery and Hiram out of love of the enslaved. Corrine is playing a 'long game,' and as part of her planning has arranged for Sophia to be kept safe from Nathaniel; Hiram feels that action must be taken immediately because the only real safety for Sophia and Thena lies in the North. On the other hand, one could say that, despite her appeals to reason, Corrine is the one whose judgment is clouded by emotion. Hiram observes that Corrine is "among the most fanatical agents I ever encountered," adding that all white agents are fanatical in their fight against slavery because, "Slavery humiliated them, because it offended a basic sense of goodness that they believed themselves to possess" (370). In their argument, both are "speaking in full faith and honesty," but they are seeing things from two entirely different perspectives (373). The fact that the narrative exposes the complex, human and flawed motivations of those who risk their lives in resisting slavery is a mark of the novel's maturity.

It is interesting that Hiram breaks off his account of his bitter argument with Corrine. He explains, "I hold her, all these years later, in the highest respect" (373) and earlier wrote, "I could not see the genius of it, not at the time, for we were, even if united in our goal, too much committed to opposing routes" (368). This suggests that, in the years between the events recorded in his narrative and the publication of that narrative, he learns something of Corrine's wider plans and that changed his opinion of her.

Chapter XXXII

Guiding Questions:
81. Explain how water dancing is linked to Conduction.
82. What are Hiram's plans for Sophia and Carrie once he has liberated them? How does Sophia react when she learns what his plans are?
83. Explain Thena's reaction to Hiram telling her that he has met her daughter and intends to reunite them.

Summary:

Forced to save Sophia and Thena using his power of Conduction rather than the agents of the Underground, Hiram realizes that he will have to tell them exactly what he proposes to do and how he proposes to do it. One night, he finally tells Sophia the whole story of his year away. She is shocked and somewhat resentful that he left her in Lockless, but Hiram assures her that he always meant to come to free her, and she trusts him, even if she is unsure of Corrine and the other Underground agents. When she asks how they will escape, Hiram takes her to the Goose and begins talking about the Christmas before their escape attempt. Conduction results: visions of those past days appear, and the two are transported to the other side of the riverbank. After a few more short Conductions, Hiram transports them back to the Street. The final vision he summons is of a woman water dancing and offering someone the jar to drink from.

Next night, Hiram asks Sophia about the water dance. She tells him that it originates in a traditional story of an African king who was brought to America on a slave ship with his people. They killed the white crew and tried to turn the ship around to sail back to Africa, but it ran aground. Quickly surrounded by an army of whites, the king told his people to walk out onto the water and to sing and dance as they did so, promising that the water goddess would take them back to Africa. Hiram links this story to that of Santi Bess who led slaves dancing into the River Goose. He admits to Sophia that knowing of his power of Conduction was why Corrine wanted him to be an Underground agent.

They discuss Hiram's plans to use Conduction to get Sophia and Carrie out. One problem Hiram has not resolved is that he needs a deeper memory, and needs an object linked to that memory, for the Conduction to operate over a great distance. Sophia asks what plans Hiram has for her and Carrie, and he replies that he must stay in Elm County but will set her up somewhere safe and visit when he can. Sophia states that she will not go without him, "'I have lived here so long watching these families go to pieces. And here I have formed one, with you, with a man who is … [Carrie's] daddy, more of a daddy than that girl would ever have'" (380-381). Hiram tells her that she is "'chaining'" herself, but she replies, "'Ain't a chain if it is my choosing'" (381).

Thena and Hiram spend the next day together doing the laundry, Sophia having feigned an illness to Carrie to give them time together. Having failed to find a way to introduce the topic gently, Hiram abruptly tells Thena that he has seen her daughter Kessiah, that she lives free outside Philadelphia with a husband who loves her, and that he has promised to take Thena to her. Thena is shocked: she recalls memories of Kessiah as a small child; she wails and moans; finally, she becomes angry because Hiram has stirred up a sadness that it had cost her so much emotionally to make peace with. Then, Thena rushes off into the night shouting that she is done with Hiram.

Hiram reflects that he understands Thena's reluctance to remember her lost daughter – after all, he himself has blocked out all memories of his lost mother.

Analysis:

Finally, Hiram has no alternative but to share the full truth first with Sophia and then with Thena. Until now, he has put his obligation to Corrine and the Underground ahead of his personal obligation to the three people he loves, but now that must end since he needs to get them to safety before that becomes impossible.

Hiram's demonstration of Conduction to Sophia makes it clear to her both why Corrine considered him to be so important to the Underground and how he plans to get her and her daughter to freedom. To be honest, Sophia takes the experience of being teleported across a river rather calmly! To some extent this is explained because the experience is not unfamiliar. Hiram tells her, "'It's like dancing'" – which we know she is very good at (378). In fact, it is Sophia who is able to make the connection for Hiram (and the reader) between the traditional water dance and the Conductions of the African King and of Santi Bess. The water dance is a ritual the full meaning of which, like many old rituals, has been lost to the people who practice it. Water dancing is an expression of the revolt of black people against their enslavement.

Typically, Hiram has decided on the future of Sophia and their daughter without consulting her. (Men!) However, Sophia makes it clear that she will decide her own future: if Hiram is going to stay in Elm County because of his commitment to Corrine, then she and Carrie will stay there too. Sophia has been separated from one husband by slavery and, having built with Hiram a new family unit, one in which the three of them are linked by blood, she will not be part of breaking it up. Paradoxically, she will be Hiram's because he has learned that she is *not* his, and she will assert her freedom by *choosing* to stay with him in Lockless in the capacity of a slave.

The scene in which Hiram tells Thena about having met her daughter ought to be one of joy, but it is not. In order to protect herself from the pain of having lost all of her children, Thena has blocked out the idea that they are still alive somewhere. Hiram brings those repressed memories flooding back. The result is that he re-traumatizes her. Today, we might diagnose Thena as suffering an attack of PTSD (post-traumatic stress disorder). Having spent decades battling flashbacks, nightmares and severe anxiety through repressing thoughts about the loss of her children, Hiram brings them flooding back in a way that is emotionally overwhelming.

Chapter XXXIII

Notes:

"Cuffee" (394): "Cuffee or Cuffey is a first name recorded in African-American culture, believed to be derived from the Akan language name Kofi, meaning 'born on a Friday'. This was noted as one of the most common male names of African origin which was retained by some American slaves." (Wikipedia contributors. "Cuffee." *Wikipedia, The Free Encyclopedia.* Wikipedia, The Free Encyclopedia, 14 Oct. 2018. Web. 8 Jan. 2020.)

"Mami Wata" (394): "Mami Wata (Mammy Water) is a water spirit venerated in West, Central, and Southern Africa, and in the African diaspora in the Americas … Traditions on both sides of the Atlantic tell of the spirit abducting her followers or random people whilst they are swimming or boating. She brings them to her paradisiacal realm, which may be underwater, in the spirit world, or both." (Wikipedia contributors. "Mami Wata." *Wikipedia, The Free Encyclopedia.* Wikipedia, The Free Encyclopedia, 17 Dec. 2019. Web. 8 Jan. 2020.)

Guiding Question:

84. What to you are the most shocking details of the fate of Rose that Hiram reveals during Conduction?

Summary:

The following day, Hiram writes a coded letter to the Philadelphia Underground telling Harriet what he is planning to do. Later, Hiram searches Howell's highboy and inside an ornate box finds a shell necklace which he recognizes as having seen around Rose's neck in his visions of her water dancing. Spontaneously, Hiram's repressed memories of his mother are released, and he feels the impulse to murder Howell for what he now understands him to have done. He does not do so, however, because of his obligations to Sophia and Thena. Hiram takes the necklace.

That evening, Howell has dinner with Corrine, who tells Hiram that Hawkins wants to speak to him. Hiram assumes that he is going to try to talk him out of freeing Sophia and Thena but is determined that he will not succeed. Hawkins tells Hiram that he and his sister Amy were slaves when Corrine's husband, Edmund Quinn, "'the meanest white man this world has known'" (388), was the master and that he feels gratitude and loyalty to Corrine for "'her plotting that rid us of that demon.'" As a result, he is now himself totally dedicated to, "'this new task of ridding the greater Demon he [Edmund] served'" (389). Yet Hawkins refuses to dictate what Hiram should do. The fight against the Task is a fight so that a person should be able to do what they please. Hawkins tells Hiram, "'You are free and must act according to your own sense. Can't be according to mine'" (390).

Several days later, Thena approaches Hiram. She tells him how hard his news was for her to take and how hard it had been for her to love Hiram after losing her own children and then to lose him as well. She felt "'it must be me'"; that is, she blamed herself for the loss of her children. She asks, "'What will I say to her, Hi? … What will I do when I look at her and all I can see are my lost ones?'" (391). Hiram now knows that the countdown to their last hours at Lockless has begun.

Having received no reply from Harriet after two weeks, Hiram determines to conduct Thena. He chooses a Saturday to give him Sunday to recover from the ordeal. After a final feast together, he leads Thena to the River Goose. As the fog and blue light appear, Hiram dedicates the Conduction to Rose and to all the mothers taken over the bridge to be sold, and to the mothers who remained behind after their children were so taken. Hiram then tells Thena the memory of his mother than he has finally recovered: He remembers what Rose looked like and how at night she told him stories from Africa. He recalls the "good years, under the Task" before tobacco had begun to exhaust the soil and masters in Virginia began to sell off their slaves. He remembers, just after aunt Emma had been sold, the night Rose woke him up and carried him into the forest where they evaded the slave catchers for three days. Above all, he remembers them being brought to the jail where Howell visited them, and Rose knew that he would sell her as punishment for running. She then gave the shell necklace to Hiram, telling him, "'No matter what shall happen, you are remembered to me now. Forget nothing of what you have seen … I have tried, best as I could, to be as a mother should'" (396). Then, he was literally pulled away from her and taken to Lockless where Howell took the necklace from him. Howell traded Rose for a horse, and next morning Hiram ran to the stable and by the same horse and the water trough had his first experience of Conduction. However, Hiram concludes, because, "the pain of memory, my memory so sharp and clear, was more than I could bear,'" his mind suppressed these events so that they were lost to him (397).

At this point, Conduction becomes a swirl of wordless memories. Hiram and Thena hear the voice of Harriet saying, "'It is Conduction, friend. It is the old ways, which shall and do remain'" (398). Harriet and Kessiah are standing on Delaware docks in Philadelphia, and Kessiah tells Hiram he can go back because Thena is safe with them. Through another swirl of memories, Hiram returns to Lockless.

Analysis:

Hawkins admits that Corrine is using him to try to persuade Hiram to drop his planned escape. However, despite his loyalty to Corrine and his dedication to the cause, Hawkins does not say what Corrine expects him to. Instead, he tells Hiram, "'We forget sometimes – it is freedom we are serving, it is the Task we are against. And freedom mean the right of a man to do as he please, not as we suppose'" (389-390). This is what, we have noted earlier, Corrine has lost sight of: in her way, she has taken upon herself the role of slave master over the Virginia Underground. In this, she has proved herself to be very effective, but she has lost the human dimension of her work. In passing, we should note that Hawkin's reference to Corrine "'plotting to rid us of that demon [her husband]'" certainly implies that she killed him to free the people he held in Task.

The ritual of dedicating the Conduction links the present with the past. It also links the two individuals involved in this act with the generations of those who suffered before them. The power of memory transcends space and time, and it is by the power of memory that Conduction is able to do the same for the physical body.

Hiram's recovered memories establish a connection between the old African king, Santi Bess, Harriet and himself: each has the power of Conduction which "'is the old ways, which shall and do remain'" (398). In Emma and Rose, Conduction was present only symbolically in their water dance, neither had the actual power to use memory to travel through space/time, though they shared the desire to escape and revered the power of memory. In this story, the reader can trace the generational loss of African culture and blood lineage that inevitably happened to enslaved people and their descendants in America.

Howell's crime, when we finally learn the details, is truly terrible. When he first saw his father come to the jail, Hiram actually believed than he had come to free them. However, when Rose would not say why she ran, "'his pained look twisted into a rage ... my mother had seen through all the noble façade, and she knew what he was – this was what her flight meant – that she understood...'" (397). Thus, Howell acted so viciously out of personal revenge. Readers have been prepared for this because the narrative has continuously stressed the self-deceptive hypocrisy of the Quality – their need to believe in their own benevolence in a brutal, exploitative system.

Chapter XXXIV

Guiding Question:
85. What do you understand by Sophia's statement that concludes this chapter and the novel?

Summary:
Hiram wakes in an unfamiliar bed and falls to the floor when he tries to get up. Hawkins comes in and explains that Sophia found Hiram outside her cabin on Sunday morning, shivering with fever. She sent word to Corrine who had him brought to the Starfall Inn. Later, when he is somewhat recovered, Corrine expresses disapproval at what Hiram has done because it could pose problems for the Virginia Underground. In response, Hiram insists that "'this Conduction, it belongs to something older than the Underground. And as sure as I must be loyal to you, I have got to be loyal to that'" (401). He adds that if he has to Conduct Sophia to save her, then he will do so because she has saved him twice. Corrine calmly replies that she will have to make sure that the need does not arise. Only a year later does Hiram understand Corrine's meaning. Howell dies in the fall, and Lockless becomes Corrine's property. The remaining slaves are secretly sent to freedom in the North, and agents replace them in what soon becomes another station of the Underground with Hiram in charge.

When he returns to Lockless, Hiram makes sure that Howell sees him wearing Rose's necklace. He is not interested in his father's response, Hiram just wants "him to know that I now knew all that he knew, that to forgive was irrelevant, but to forget was death" (403). That night, Hiram asks Sophia, "'What are we now?'" and she replies, "'We are what we always were ... Underground'" (403).

Analysis:
The Water Dancer appears to have a conventional ending – love triumphs. The reader certainly does not begrudge Thena and Kessiah the happiness they have found; it comes after years of pain. Will Otha ever find happiness with Lydia? We do not know. Happiness in this novel is rare and temporary. This is also true of Hiram and Sophia. Hiram (like a knight in a medieval quest) has finally proved himself worthy of Sophia by recognizing in himself the male impulse to control and master the female, which is not much different from the white impulse to control and master the black. Both remain in the South, doing the dangerous work of securing freedom for others. We remember also that the Civil War is imminent (something about which the characters themselves are obviously unaware) and they will be trapped on the Confederate side in that conflict. Wamuwi Mbao finds the unresolved conclusion disappointing, arguing that, "because the novel builds itself around the idea that Hiram will become the hero, you expect that everything will synthesise [sic] into one cohesive narrative ... It's an extraordinarily frustrating anticlimax, but one that suggests that remaking the country can only be accomplished by remaking the memories that are embedded in the soil."

Perspectives

The Water Dancer, Coates' meditation on the legacy of slavery, is a work of both staggering imagination and rich historical significance. (David Fear)

This modern masterpiece enables us to comprehend what it must be to have never known freedom and risk everything to attain it. (Leigh Haber)

In *Between the World and Me*, which took the form of a letter to his son, Coates observed: "Slavery is not an indefinable mass of flesh. It is a particular, specific enslaved woman, whose mind is active as your own, whose range of feeling is as vast as your own." One of his achievements in this novel is to closely underscore the human particularity of a range of enslaved men and women. (Dwight Garner)

Coates's debut novel has exquisite sentences and ideas, but the rest is a mess … Ta-Nehisi Coates is not yet a great novelist … Ta-Nehisi Coates is not quite there yet. He doesn't have the kind of command over the novel as a medium that will let him meld disparate genres together; he doesn't seem to care about his characters as people rather than as devices he can use to convey ideas; he doesn't really understand how to keep a plot moving. (Constance Grady)

At its best, *The Water Dancer* is a melancholic and suspenseful novel that merges the slavery narrative with the genres of fantasy or quest novels. But moments of great lyricism are matched with clichés and odd narrative gaps, and the mechanics of plot sometimes seem to grind and stall. (Annalisa Quinn)

It's not a stretch to see in Coates's harrowing descriptions here the caged children of migrants who may never see their parents again, lost in a system that sees them as less than human. (Renée Graham Globe)

Ultimately, while the plot does work on both a profound level and a page-turner level – for *Water Dancer* remains, while chock full of ideas, immensely readable – the skill Coates most brings to the table here, which was present in his nonfiction work, is his ability to craft individual sentences on a rare level. (Luke Murphy)

The book's most poignant and painful gift is the temporary fantasy that all the people who leaped off slave ships and into the Atlantic were not drowning themselves in terror and anguish, but going home. (Annalisa Quinn)

[A]s promising as the idea of magic is, and the attached metaphor of Hiram not being able to come into the extent of his power until he accepts his history, it is at times a clunky, unwieldy presence in the book. The few times the novel does veer off the train tracks, losing its footing tonally, is when magic comes into play. That is not to say it doesn't work at all, for it often does, but the presence of literal magic does not work with the consistency of the story of Hiram and Sophia or Hiram and his relationships with people in the Underground. (Luke Murphy)

The Water Dancer builds itself around the tension of Hiram learning how to

The Water Dancer by Ta-Nehisi Coates

Conduct, and it imbues that problem with a kind of comic book pulpiness: There are glowing lights and training montages, and also Harriet Tubman shows up to do a little glowing of her own. (Constance Grady)

An almost-but-not-quite-great slavery novel. (Kirkus Review)

[A]n underlying message of liberation through the embrace of history forms the true subject of *The Water Dancer* ... instead of imagining a literal railroad in place of a treacherous, multi-stop effort to pull innocent people from the depths of slavery, Coates envisions the transcendent potential in acknowledging and retelling stories of trauma from the past as a means out of darkness. With recent family separations at the U.S. border, this message feels all the more timely. (Chris Barton)

The Water Dancer is at once a painful catalog of the evils and repercussions of slavery and a powerful and mystical explanation of how African American captives managed to free themselves from their chains. (Nancy Gibson)

[A]t its core, *The Water Dancer* is a love story. And I thought it would be really cool to set a love story during that period. Letters from wives to husbands or husbands to wives where their loved ones were about to be sold off ... were just some of the most affecting notes that I read. (Coates in an interview with Hannah Giorgis)

Even as Hiram embarks on a sort of Horatio Alger adventure from the repressive South to the free North via the Underground Railroad, encountering heroes and villains and becoming an integral member of the resistance along the way, the plot gets lodged in digressions and cul-de-sacs — leaning heavily on blue-mist atmosphere and characters who speak less like humans than oracles in long, lyrical turns. (Leah Greenblatt)

Yes, the novel, *The Water Dancer*, was picked by Oprah Winfrey for her much-prized book club, and it has received rave reviews in a number of places, but the truth is it's pretty much a mess from beginning to end. (Charles Mudede)

Bibliography

Coates, Ta-Nehisi. *The Water Dancer: A Novel*. New York: One World, 2019. Print.

Anon. "*The Water Dancer* Ta-Nehisi Coates." *Best Books, Authors*, Publishers Weekly. 6 Nov. 2019. Web. 22 Nov. 2019.

Ajayi, Angela. "Review: *The Water Dancer*, by Ta-Nehisi Coates." *Fiction*, Star Tribune. 20 Sep. 2019. Web. 22 Nov. 2019.

Anon. "*The Water Dancer* by Ta-Nehisi Coates." *Kirkus Reviews*, Kirkus 24 Sep. 2019. Web. 22 Nov. 2019.

Barton, Chris. "Review: Ta-Nehisi Coates imagines a magical means to freedom." *Books*, The Los Angeles Times. 22 Sep. 2019. Web. 22 Nov. 2019.

Capossere, Bill. "The Water Dancer: Sharply moving but also oddly distant." *SFF Reviews*, Fantasy Literature. 12 Nov. 2019. Web. 16 Jan. 2020.

Charles, Ron. "In Ta-Nehisi Coates's *The Water Dancer*, a slave makes a superhero's journey." *Books*, The Washington Post. 23 Sep. 2019. Web. 23 Nov. 2019.

Coard, Michael. "American Slavery Was Born 393 Years Ago Today." *News and Opinion*, Philadelphia Magazine. 20 Aug. 2012. Web. 10 Jan. 2020.

Domise, Andre. "Ta-Nehisi Coates's book *The Water Dancer* focuses on the power of stories." *Book Review*, The Globe and Mail. 1 Oct. 2019. Web. 16 Jan. 2020.

Fear, David. "*The Water Dancer*: Ta-Nehisi Coates' American Odyssey" *Culture Features*, Rolling Stone. 24 Sep. 2019. Web. 19 Nov. 2019.

Garner, Dwight. "With *The Water Dancer*, Ta-Nehisi Coates Makes His Fiction Debut." *Books of the Times*, The New York Times. 20 Sep. 2019. Web. 15 Jan. 2020.

Gaylord, Joan. "Aching and perceptive, *The Water Dancer* is an essential read." *The Christian Science Monitor*. 17 Oct. 2019. Web. 27 Nov. 2019.

Gilson, Nancy. "Book review: *The Water Dancer*: Ta-Nehisi Coates' tale of Underground Railroad rich in detail." *Entertainment and Life*, The Columbus Dispatch. 29 Sep. 2019. Web. 27 Nov. 2019.

Giorgis, Hannah. "What Ta-Nehisi Coates Wants to Remember." *The Atlantic*. 29 Sep. 2019. Web. 27 Nov. 2019.

Grady, Constance. "Ta-Nehisi Coates is a great writer. His new book *The Water Dancer* is not a great novel." Vox. 24. Sep. 2019. Web. 22 Nov. 2019.

Graham, Renée. "*The Water Dancer* is an electrifying debut novel from Ta-Nehisi Coates." *Book Review*, Boston Globe. 26 Sept. 2019. Web. 29 Nov. 2019.

Greenblatt, Leah. "Ta-Nehisi Coates' debut novel is a magical, gorgeously evocative achievement." *Book Reviews*, Entertainment.16 Sep. 2019. Web. 14 Jan.

2020.

Gross, Terry. "Ta-Nehisi Coates On Magic, Memory And The Underground Railroad." *Author Interviews*, NPR. 24 Sep. 2019. Web. 14 Jan. 2020.

Haber, Leigh. "Origin Story." *Oprah Magazine*. Oct. 2019: 101. Print.

Mbao, Wamuwi. "A depth charge aimed at the submerged wreckage of slavery." The Johannesburg Review of Books. 4 Nov. 2019. Web. 15 Jan. 2020.

McMichael, Shaun. "Discovering Family, Memory, and Teleportation in Ta-Nehisi Coates' *The Water Dancer*." *Books*, Pop Matters. 29 Oct. 2019. Web. 27 Nov. 2019.

"Memory is a superpower in Ta-Nehisi Coates' novel about the Underground Railroad." *PBS News Hour Transcript*, PBS. 24 Sep. 2019. Web. 14 Jan. 2020.

Mobray, Beth. "Review: *The Water Dancer* by Ta-Nehisi Coates." Books, The Nerd Daily. 20 Oct. 2019. Web. 15 Jan. 2020.

Mudede, Charles. "Ta-Nehisi Coates Is Not Perfect." *Books*, The Stranger. p Oct. 2019. Web. 15 Jan. 2020.

Murphy, Luke. "Review: Ta-Nehisi Coates's debut novel *The Water Dancer*." *Arts/Life*, The DePaulia. 21 Oct. 2019. Web. 29 Nov. 2019.

Quinn, Annalisa. "In *The Water Dancer*, Ta-Nehisi Coates Creates Magical Alternate History." Book Reviews, NPR. 26 Sep. 2019. Wed. 21 Nov. 2019.

An Ongoing Battle

Rodriques, Elias. "Ta-Nehisi Coates's narratives of freedom." *Fiction*, The Nation. 29 Oct. 2019. Web. 15 Jan. 2020.

Seresin, Indiana. "*The Water Dancer*". *LitCharts*. LitCharts LLC, 24 Oct 2019. Web. 31 Dec 2019.

Wikipedia contributors. "William Still." *Wikipedia, The Free Encyclopedia*. Wikipedia, The Free Encyclopedia, 9 Dec. 2019. Web. 12 Jan. 2020.

Appendix 1: Reading Group Use of the Study Guide Questions

Although there are both closed and open questions in the Study Guide, very few of them have simple, right or wrong answers. They are designed to encourage in-depth discussion, disagreement, and (eventually) consensus. Above all, they aim to encourage readers to go to the text to support their conclusions and interpretations.

I am not so arrogant as to presume to tell readers how they should use this resource. I used it in the following ways, each of which ensured that group members were well prepared for group discussion and presentations.

1. Set a reading assignment for the group and tell everyone to be aware that the questions will be the focus of whole group discussion at the next meeting.

2. Set a reading assignment for the group and allocate particular questions to sections of the group (e.g. if there are four questions, divide the group into four sections, etc.).
In the meeting, form discussion groups containing one person who has prepared each question and allow time for feedback within the groups.
Have feedback to the whole the on each question by picking a group at random to present their answers and to follow up with a group discussion.

3. Set a reading assignment for the group, but do not allocate questions.
In the meeting, divide readers into groups and allocate to each group one of the questions related to the reading assignment, the answer to which they will have to present formally to the meeting.
Allow time for discussion and preparation.

4. Set a reading assignment for the group, but do not allocate questions.
In the meeting, divide readers into groups and allocate to each group one of the questions related to the reading assignment.
Allow time for discussion and preparation.
Now reconfigure the groups so that each group contains at least one person who has prepared each question and allow time for feedback within the groups.

5. Before starting to read the text, allocate specific questions to individuals or pairs. (It is best not to allocate all questions to allow for other approaches and variety. One in three questions or one in four seems about right.) Tell readers that they will be leading the group discussion on their question. They will need to start with a brief presentation of the issues and then conduct a question and answer session. After this, they will be expected to present a brief review of the discussion.

The Water Dancer by Ta-Nehisi Coates

6. Having finished the text, arrange the meeting into groups of 3, 4 or 5. Tell each group to select as many questions from the Study Guide as there are members of the group.

Each individual is responsible for drafting out an answer to one question, and each answer should be substantial.

Each group as a whole is then responsible for discussing, editing and suggesting improvements to each answer.

Appendix 2: Literary Terms

Ambiguous, ambiguity: when a statement is unclear in meaning – ambiguity may be deliberate or accidental.

Analogy: a comparison which treats two things as identical in one or more specified ways.

Antagonist: a character or force opposing the protagonist.

Antithesis: the complete opposite of something.

Climax: the conflict to which the action has been building since the start of the play or story.

Colloquialism: the casual, informal mainly spoken language of ordinary people – often called "slang."

Connotation: the ideas, feelings and associations generated by a word or phrase.

Dark comedy: comedy which has a serious implication – comedy that deals with subjects not usually treated humorously (e.g., death).

Dialogue: a conversation between two or more people in direct speech.

Diction: the writer's choice of words in order to create a particular effect.

Equivocation: saying something which is capable of two interpretations with the intention of misrepresenting the truth.

Euphemism: a polite word for an ugly truth – for example, a person is said to be sleeping when they are actually dead.

Fallacy: a misconception resulting from incorrect reasoning.

First person: first person singular is "I" and plural is "we".

Foreshadowing: a statement or action which gives the reader a hint of what is likely to happen later in the narrative.

Genre: the type of literature into which a particular text falls (e.g. drama, poetry, novel).

Image, imagery: figurative language such as simile, metaphor, personification etc., or a description which conjures up a particularly vivid picture.

Imply, implication: when the text suggests to the reader a meaning which it does not actually state.

Infer, inference: the reader's act of going beyond what is stated in the text to draw conclusions.

Irony, ironic: a form of humor which undercuts the apparent meaning of a statement:

> **Conscious irony:** irony used deliberately by a writer or character;
>
> **Unconscious irony:** a statement or action which has significance for the reader of which the character is unaware;

Dramatic irony: when an action has an important significance that is obvious to the reader but not to one or more of the characters;

Tragic irony: when a character says (or does) something which will have a serious, even fatal, consequence for him/ her. The audience is aware of the error, but the character is not;

Verbal irony: the conscious use of particular words which are appropriate to what is being said.

Juxtaposition: literally putting two things side by side for purposes of comparison and/ or contrast.

Literal: the surface level of meaning that a statement has.

Melodramatic: action and/or dialogue that is inflated or extravagant – frequently used for comic effect.

Metaphor, metaphorical: the description of one thing by direct comparison with another (e.g. the coal-black night).

Extended metaphor: a comparison which is developed at length.

Mood: the feelings and emotions contained in and/ or produced by a work of art (text, painting, music, etc.).

Motif: a frequently repeated idea, image or situation in a text.

Motivation: why a character acts as he/she does – in modern literature motivation is seen as psychological.

Narrator: the voice that the reader hears in the text – not to be confused with the author.

Oxymoron: the juxtaposition of two terms normally thought of as opposite (e.g. the silent scream).

Paradox, paradoxical: a statement or situation which appears self-contradictory and therefore absurd.

Pathos: is pity, or rather the ability of a text to make the audience or reader feel pity.

Perspective: point of view from which a story, or an incident within a story, is told.

Personified, personification: a simile or metaphor in which an inanimate object or abstract idea is described by comparison with a human.

Plot: a chain of events linked by cause and effect.

Protagonist: the character who initiates the action and is most likely to have the sympathy of the audience.

Realism: a text that describes the action in a way that appears to reflect life.

Sarcasm: stronger than irony – it involves a deliberate attack on a person or idea with the intention of mocking.

Setting: the environment in which the narrative (or part of the narrative) takes place.

Simile: a description of one thing by explicit comparison with another (e.g. my love is like a red, red rose).

Extended simile: a comparison which is developed at length.

Style: the way in which a writer chooses to express him/ herself. Style is a vital aspect of meaning since how something is expressed can crucially affect what is being written or spoken.

Symbol, symbolic, symbolism, symbolize: a physical object which comes to represent an abstract idea (e.g. the sun may symbolize life).

Themes: important concepts, beliefs and ideas explored and presented in a text.

Third person: third person singular is "he/ she/ it" and plural is "they" – authors often write novels in the third person.

Tone: literally the sound of a text – How words sound (either in the mouth of an actor or the head of a reader) can crucially affect meaning.

Appendix 3: Plot Graph

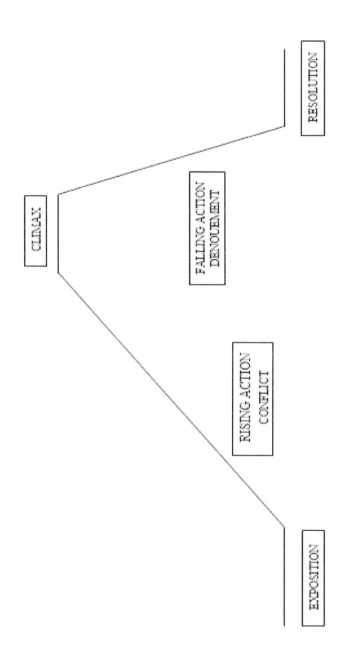

About the Author

Ray Moore was born in Nottingham, England. He obtained his Master's Degree in Literature from Lancaster University and taught in secondary education for twenty-eight years before relocating to Florida with his wife. There he taught English and Information Technology in the International Baccalaureate Program. He is now a full-time writer and fitness fanatic and leads a reading group at a local library.

Website: http://www.raymooreauthor.com

Ray strives to make his texts the best that they can be. If you have any comments or question about this book *please* contact the author through his email: **villageswriter@gmail.com**

Also, by Ray Moore:

Books are available from amazon.com and some from barnesandnoble.com as paperbacks and most are available from online eBook retailers.

Fiction:

1066: Year of the Five Kings is a novel of the most consequential year in the history of England.

The Lyle Thorne Mysteries Volumes One to Eight

Investigations of The Reverend Lyle Thorne (Volume One)

Further Investigations of The Reverend Lyle Thorne (Volume Two)

Early Investigations of Lyle Thorne (Volume Three)

Sanditon Investigations of The Rev. Lyle Thorne (Volume Four)

Final Investigations of The Rev. Lyle Thorne (Volume Five)

Lost Investigation of The Rev. Lyle Thorne (Volume Six)

Official Investigations of Lyle Thorne (Volume Seven)

Clerical Investigations of The Rev. Lyle Thorne (Volume Eight)

Non-fiction:

The **Critical Introduction series** is written for high school teachers and students and for college undergraduates. Each volume gives an in-depth analysis of a key text:

"The Stranger" by Albert Camus: A Critical Introduction (Revised Second Edition)

"The General Prologue" by Geoffrey Chaucer: A Critical Introduction

"Pride and Prejudice" by Jane Austen: A Critical Introduction

"The Great Gatsby" by F. Scott Fitzgerald: A Critical Introduction

The Text and Critical Introduction series <u>differs</u> from the Critical introduction series as these books contain the original text and in the case of the medieval texts an interlinear translation to aid the understanding of the text. The commentary allows the reader to develop a deeper understanding of the text and themes within the text.

"Sir Gawain and the Green Knight": Text and Critical Introduction*

"The General Prologue" by Geoffrey Chaucer: Text and Critical Introduction*

"Heart of Darkness" by Joseph Conrad: Text and Critical Introduction*

"Henry V" by William Shakespeare: Text and Critical Introduction*

"Oedipus Rex" by Sophocles: Text and Critical Introduction*

"A Room with a View" By E.M. Forster: Text and Critical Introduction*

Selected Poems of Robert Frost 1913-1923: Text and Critical Introduction

"The Sign of Four" by Sir Arthur Conan Doyle Text and Critical Introduction

"The Wife of Bath's Prologue and Tale" by Geoffrey Chaucer: Text and Critical Introduction*

Jane Austen: The Complete Juvenilia: Text and Critical Introduction

Study Guides - listed alphabetically by author

Study Guides offer an in-depth look at aspects of a text. They generally include an introduction to the characters, genre, themes, setting, tone of a text. They also may include activities on helpful literary terms as well as graphic organizers to aid understanding of the plot and different perspectives of characters.

* denotes also available as an eBook

"ME and EARL and the Dying GIRL" by Jesse Andrews: A Study Guide

Study Guide to "Alias Grace" by Margaret Atwood*

Study Guide to "The Handmaid's Tale" by Margaret Atwood*

"Pride and Prejudice" by Jane Austen: A Study Guide

"Moloka'i" by Alan Brennert: A Study Guide

"Wuthering Heights" by Emily Brontë: A Study Guide *

Study Guide on "Jane Eyre" by Charlotte Brontë*

"The Myth of Sisyphus" by Albert Camus: A Study Guide

"The Stranger" by Albert Camus: A Study Guide

"The Myth of Sisyphus" and "The Stranger" by Albert Camus: Two Study Guides *

Study Guide to "Death Comes to the Archbishop" by Willa Cather

"The Awakening" by Kate Chopin: A Study Guide

Study Guide to Seven Short Stories by Kate Chopin

Study Guide to "Ready Player One" by Ernest Cline

Study Guide to "Disgrace" by J. M. Coetzee

The Water Dancer by Ta-Nehisi Coates

"The Meursault Investigation" by Kamel Daoud: A Study Guide

Study Guide on "Great Expectations" by Charles Dickens*

"The Sign of Four" by Sir Arthur Conan Doyle: A Study Guide *

Study Guide to "Manhattan Beach" by Jennifer Egan

"The Wasteland, Prufrock and Poems" by T.S. Eliot: A Study Guide

Study Guide on "Birdsong" by Sebastian Faulks*

"The Great Gatsby" by F. Scott Fitzgerald: A Study Guide

"A Room with a View" by E. M. Forster: A Study Guide

Study Guide with Text to "Selected Poems 1913-1923" by Robert Frost

"Looking for Alaska" by John Green: A Study Guide

"Paper Towns" by John Green: A Study Guide

Study Guide to "Turtles All the Way Down" by John Green

Study Guide to "Florida" by Lauren Groff

Study Guide on "Catch-22" by Joseph Heller *

"Unbroken" by Laura Hillenbrand: A Study Guide

"The Kite Runner" by Khaled Hosseini: A Study Guide

"A Thousand Splendid Suns" by Khaled Hosseini: A Study Guide

Study Guide with Text to "A Shropshire Lad" by A. E. Housman

"The Secret Life of Bees" by Sue Monk Kidd: A Study Guide

Study Guide on "The Invention of Wings" by Sue Monk Kidd

Study Guide to "Fear and Trembling" by Søren Kierkegaard

"Go Set a Watchman" by Harper Lee: A Study Guide

Study Guide to "Pachinko" by Min Jin Lee

"On the Road" by Jack Kerouac: A Study Guide

Study Guide on "Life of Pi" by Yann Martel*

Study Guide to "Death of a Salesman" by Arthur Miller

Study Guide to "The Bluest Eye" by Toni Morrison

Study Guide to "Reading Lolita in Tehran" by Azir Nafisi

Study Guide to "The Sympathizer" by Viet Thanh Nguyen

"Animal Farm" by George Orwell: A Study Guide

Study Guide on "Nineteen Eighty-Four" by George Orwell

Study Guide to "The Essex Serpent" by Sarah Perry

Study Guide to "Selected Poems" and Additional Poems by Sylvia Plath*

"An Inspector Calls" by J.B. Priestley: A Study Guide

New titles are added regularly.

Readers' Guides

Readers' Guides offer an introduction to important aspects of the text and questions for personal reflection and/or discussion. Guides are written for individual readers who wish to explore texts in depth and for members of Reading Circles who wish to make their discussions of texts more productive.

The Water Dancer by Ta-Nehisi Coates
A Reader's Guide to Becoming by Michelle Obama
A Reader's Guide to Educated: A Memoir by Tara Westover

Teacher resources: Ray also publishes many more study guides and other resources for classroom use on the 'Teachers Pay Teachers' website: **http://www.teacherspayteachers.com/Store/Raymond-Moore**

Made in the USA
Monee, IL
09 May 2021